7 Steps to Realign Body, Soul, Spirit

Michal Russo

D1713731

DEDICATION

First and foremost, I dedicate this book to The One and only, Our Father in heaven, Creator of all things: All of creation and creativity, all goodness, all that we have come to know or claim to ever know and understand, and that which we do not. The Savior of my soul, and The One that I want to walk with for the rest of my days.

Secondly, I dedicate this book to YOU, each and every one of you reading this. In it, you will take a deep dive inward, where we walk through a journey together, step by step, towards realigning body, soul, and spirit in Christ. I share my past story and experience of fighting to do life my own way in the New Age, culminating in my utter "crash and burn", and finally, my complete surrender to the cross. My hope is that you may also enjoy the peace, love, and joy that surpasses all understanding which I have received through Him, and avoid the traps and snares that led me down a slippery slope to devastation. I hope that you will take the wisdom and revelations that God downloads to you in your own life through journeying these steps as you experience this life, and to eternity thereafter. He is The (only) Way, the (only) Truth, and The (only) Life.

CONTENTS

FOREWORD

I want to start out by congratulating you on having the bold bravery to seek Truth as you embark on a journey of alignment in Faith, by Grace. Many of us start out well-intentioned on the path to seeking our destiny and purpose. Most of us didn't see when we had taken a wrong turn. It happens subtly and quickly, and one wrong turn at a time doesn't really feel all that wrong. Until, if you're like me, several wrong turns later, we wake up and realize we'd completely lost our way. We feel disconnected from the world we have created around us. We feel empty, regardless of how many people or things we have acquired, or how many trophies of success we have in the closet. We are left with an ever-gaping sense of wanting something more. For me, it took a total "crash and burn" moment to finally realize I had fallen from His Perfect Plan for me. It took reckless abandonment and isolation for me to surrender my will, my plan, and my idea of my own self-purpose, back over to Him. I really didn't want to let go of the wheel for the sake of fear, failure, betrayal, and loss of control. What I didn't know though, or refused to acknowledge, was that while I clung desperately to the wheel, every single stop and turn along that route was only leading me further down a path colored in all of those dark things. And, they were only getting darker the longer I reluctantly pursued life my own way.

It can take a lot for us to admit that we may be stumbling down a wayward path, or headed the wrong way. Some of us stick stubbornly to it for years, in the hopes that we might eventually muster the strength to win something worth claiming victory over, something that redeems us. Meanwhile, all this time, our entire beings, (body, soul, and spirit) are desperately craving alignment.

There is one way, however, that I know works, and that's called complete surrender. Sounds ironic when I had lived a life brimming with a tough girl mindset of "I'll fight my own battles". It really was after a lifetime low that I realized I was never actually going to "be enough" on my own, and that was okay. I did not need to be perfect, nor would I ever be... and that didn't come from piety, or pride. No, I found my strength in complete brokenness. It took me completely shattering to see The Light through the cracks and decide I didn't need to, or couldn't possibly ever put myself back together. So, I let Him.

The best part is... God is The Master at meeting us exactly where we are at. He doesn't require a certain number of Sundays with your butt in the pew to hear you. He doesn't demand a certain number of prayers or rituals a day for Him to shine His face towards you. His specialty happens to be picking up those who are face flat on the floor, and turning their faces towards Him.

He heals the broken-hearted and binds up their wounds. Psalm 147:3

My Personal Journey

I have been described as quite a few things in this life, and most of them are adjectives that I would never put to writing down here. I am grateful to God for what He has delivered me from, and I do open up about much of it in these pages. However, the final tipping point that led me to what I call my great "crash and burn" was perhaps the most subtle of deceptions. I became fully entrapped, and it wasn't drugs and alcohol, although those played their destructive parts in my past too, but something that came cloaked in light, and something that I had come to believe as "good". It was my former career as a yoga teacher. Through practicing and teaching yoga, I thought I was contributing to the overall positive well-being of myself and others. I was in pursuit of calm, peace and tranquility. This was the way, I thought. So, I began to study it, and not just any form, I began in a studio that observed the Bikram College of India way. I was told, in this small Bikram studio in Miami, Florida, the whole theory of 90 minutes in this heated room was better than an eternity in hell. My emancipation and salvation would come after Savasana, or the final resting "dead man's pose", and I thought nothing more of this, even then, even as a believer. I was also barked at for attempting to drink water in between poses, and told my shorts and mat were the wrong color and draining positive energy from the rest of that class, so I should not return with them again. After two years of Bikram, I ventured into different styles of yoga. Over the next decade I dabbled in Iyengar, Ashtanga, Power, and Yin Yoga, and eventually found my favorite style was Hatha Vinyasa. Hatha Vinyasa is a style that combines movement with breath as a form of meditation across poses. So, after over a decade of avidly practicing yoga, I finally embarked on a trip overseas to get my yoga teacher training. I sought out more than just another teacher to guide me through this process, I wanted a guru. I got my 200hr RYTT teaching certificate in Hatha Vinyasa, and my Yoga Alliance membership, and started offering classes as soon as I got back to the United States. I did this by teaching at private studios and on a military base to soldiers and their families. Again, I thought I was helping people. Helping them relieve pain, stress, tension, and recover from PTSD. I didn't realize, or want to realize, the spiritual parts I was imparting them with, even though I kept it pretty watered down when I led the classes through ohms, chants, asanas, meditations, and mudras. I maintained that they were helpful and harmless, even though they often directly called out "auspicious goodness", Shiva, and other God's by name. I thought that when I eventually put a buddha in my home, it was harmless. After all, we had them in the studio and whenever I asked or was asked about them, we would just say they "represent peace", rather than recognizing it for what it was: blatant idolatry and worship of a false god. Or, when I eventually built a small altar in my basement with my yogic books, chakra stones, guides and incense, I convinced myself that it wasn't wrong again. When I wore "yoga pants" I never thought twice about what I was truly calling them. When I bowed down on my yoga mat, I never considered myself bowing down to other God's or submitting myself in connection by yoking to anything at all... I was just breathing and stretching... right?

This wasn't, and isn't, an easy assignment, answering the call by God to share my story of crashing and burning that led me to a total realignment of body, soul, and spirit in Faith and by Grace. The further I pursued the Faith, the block came. Like a physical & spiritual stop sign that no longer allowed me to continue practicing yoga let alone teach it. Like any ritual that you practice so often it becomes automatic, yoga had become my whole world. From my career, to yogi friends, to my actual identity; it involved my entire body and soul, and unknowingly my spirit too. I longed for that time where I felt like I was flowing, and like I was aligned, often how I had convinced myself I felt during yoga. I knew I needed a complete restoration, from the inside-out, and that it had to involve more than just my body and soul now, because my spirit had finally been awakened to what it had been yoking to, and it was not Christ. I will go into more depth on the truth about yoga later in this book, as it took me certain steps that I had to reach first to accept this knowledge and I realize that it may also be that way for you too. I want to be clear and intentional about my faith, and His sweet mercy and grace. I knew I wanted to help others by sharing my experience so that they could find restoration and realignment in faith, by grace.

1 AWAKEN

First things first, I think it's important to discuss what we are seeking alignment in, and why. In the New Age world that I was not just living in, but teaching in, we often referred to our complete beings as "body, mind, and soul". It was not until I took a deeper dive in my Faith in Christ that I realized these words were redundant and not how He had intended us to operate. They were missing the most important component: Him. Perhaps this was part of the reason that no matter how many days I practiced yoga, spent hours in worldly meditation or being mindful, I was still incredibly misaligned.

Body, Soul, and Spirit

The Bible says our beings are perfectly made of body, soul and spirit:

"May your whole spirit, soul and body be preserved blameless at the coming of our Lord Jesus." 1 Thessalonians 5:23.

In this scripture, Paul delivers a powerful perspective of what our beings look like. Our bodies are materially evident, and their care and management are more or less instinctual. We eat when we are hungry, we cease action when the body alarms us with pain, we sleep when we are tired, and so on. The soul and the spirit however, are immaterial and therefore require a more conscious and intentional effort to maintain them. The Greek word used in 1 Thessalonians 5:23 for the soul is "psuche" and it implies our mind, our will and our emotions. This is where our personality traits, desires, and our personal will dwells.

When a baby is born, they have the most pure and innocent essence about them, don't they? They are completely pure in body and soul. Not long after birth, their little personalities begin to develop and evolve. It is ever so obvious when their quirks and coos, which delights the parents and all of those around them to watch and see, start to blossom into their own unique identities and personalities at young ages. Alas, the world around them is highly influential. They learn how to talk and express emotion based on others around them. They react to situations by mimicking how they see others behave. Thus, it is vitally best to have a safe, stable, and nurturing environment when raising little ones. We care for the development of their little bodies and we want them to have every opportunity to start life off right, and as blissfully happy souls. If only we, as adults, kept such careful care of our own environments once we evolved enough in body and soul to be on our own. I will be the first to admit that I rebelled against this type of environment, and it threw me astray for decades, mostly because I was spiritually dead.

The Greek word for spirit is "pneuma" and it implies the most vital source of our beings, the part that connects us to God. Our spirit is where and how we communicate with Him. It is the deepest aspect of our being and what gives us the ability to commune with God The Father. So while we are developed in body and soul, we can still completely lack the one and only aspect of our creation that gives us the identity of being a "child of God". Without this part of us active and alive in Him (Jesus Christ The Son), we have no hope for redemption of sin, and no ability to seek divine guidance and supernatural help from The Holy Spirit (His Helper). For God created us in His very image. He is three in one: Father, Son, and Holy Spirit. He created us with these three distinct things: body, soul and spirit. When they are not active and awake in Him, we fall naturally out of our intended alignment. This is what I had so dangerously done when yoking to other gods and spirits through my mantras, chants, and even bodily worship (poses) in yoga.

So, you see, if the word "mind" is not being used to describe our literal brain matter, but rather what is encompassed in our souls (I.e. our

2

personality traits, emotions, personal desires, and will), then saying the words "body" (material), "mind" (immaterial) and "soul" (immaterial) is like saying the word "soul" twice and leaving out the most divinely deep aspect of our creations that connects us to God: our spirits.

As born-again believers we become spiritually awake, and we receive yet another gift that intertwines with our spirit, and it is The Holy Spirit. He is a promised and cherished gift that keeps giving, and He comes to dwell within us, co-mingling and guiding our human spirit:

"The Spirit Himself witnesses with our spirit that we are children of God," Romans 8:6.

In 1 Corinthians 6:17, Paul said, *"But he who is joined to the Lord is one spirit."*

Choose Who You Serve

Sometimes it can be hard to tell whether we're living and doing things in our soul, or in our spirit. This is a key difference from how my former self used to strive to live in "body, mind, and soul". I was not even seeking spirit, or His spirit. I was living a life where I was choosing to serve "my higher self", and I was not even seeking His will, His divine purpose, or His plan for me. I had also opened up all of my spiritual gates to other gods and spirits, who began to wreak havoc across all aspects of my life. I refused to recognize it at the time, because I was convinced that it all simply wasn't wrong. I was deceived to believe that my behavior in body and soul could coexist with the faith I had once clung to in Christ. I later found out that was completely syncretic, but not until after the damage was done. As yoga teachers we would often default to diluting any religion from our practice by calling whatever god or spirit we were consenting to at the time our "Higher Power". On these days, my highest power was my "higher-self", and that led to some really catastrophic problems I not only created (and often with good intentions), but ultimately crashed and burned in. You see, what I had gotten myself into, I unsurprisingly had very little help or knowledge of how to get out of.

3

Perhaps you can relate? Have you ever found yourself in situations where you find yourself wondering, "How did I end up here?", or "How could they have done this to me", or "How could I let this happen", only to realize you ended up there at your own will, whether it be stubborn or completely lacking any direction, and you were the only one to blame? These were the "walls" I had come to hit often, and I was finally fed up.

I was operating solely in the realm of my own creation, instead of acknowledging all that was around me as His creation, and myself as a child of God. From my perspective, where the world around me was what I had created and a result of my decisions and actions, it really did look like a dismal existence with limited beliefs of false hopes, desperate dreams, and a finite life, not to mention my own pitiful "self-worship". How much easier it is to rejoice in the knowledge that He has already prepared everything good to come before me, and has given me eternal life!? I rejoice that He loves me and accepts me as broken as I am, and that all I need to do is trust Him as my Savior, while I seek to hear and obey Him.

"He predestined us to adoption as sons and daughters through Jesus Christ to Himself, according to the good pleasure of His will, to the praise of the glory of His grace, with which He favored us in the Beloved." Ephesians 1:516

Learning to Hear God

How we hear God is one of my most favorite aspects of having fellowship, and how it evolves with consistent communion in an intimate relationship with Him. My teenage son recently asked me how I know when I hear God's voice, and how he could too. It was such a treasure and privilege to go on a month or so long learning expedition where we sent articles, devotions, and blogs back and forth as he developed this knowledge and began to intentionally practice both talking to God and listening to Him speak.

I will share with you now what I shared with him, and the first place to start is by meditating on the written word of God:

In the beginning was the Word, and the Word was with God, and the Word was God. John 1:1

John used the Greek word "logos" here to imply that God's Word was more than just ideas or speech written on paper. The term "logos" also implies His divine reason implicit in the cosmos, ordering it and giving it form and meaning.[1] Therefore, His logos word can also be understood as the very essence of God Himself, and as His divine reason that gave the very order of things in the universe and spoke life as we know it into existence. The very power of creation, originating from His Words being released. It's an astounding revelation to look around us and think, every single thing we have known, or ever will come to know, was created by the power of His Word, and that His Word alone contains infinite possibility and ability to accomplish that for which it was purposed.

"So shall My word be that goes forth from My mouth; It shall not return to Me void, But it shall accomplish what I please, And it shall prosper in the thing for which I sent it." Isaiah 55:11

When circumstances arise where we are unsure if God is speaking to us, we should always go to His Word first. If we look in the scriptures, we can check to see if what we think we are receiving is aligned with, or contrary to what is already written there in His Word. As we seek His Word, we can pray for Him to reveal His intended purpose to us clearly there in our spirits.

All Scripture is God-breathed and is useful for teaching, rebuking, correcting and training in righteousness, so that the servant of God may be thoroughly equipped for every good work. 2 Timothy 3:16-17

Books written by others are great, and I sure am grateful that you picked up this book, but they should be nothing more than mere stepping stones to

---

[1] "Logos". Britannica 2021 https://www.britannica.com/topic/logos (12 July 2021).

the treasure trove of truly reflecting on His Word in the scriptures. It's necessary to spend a lot of time in His Word, daily, multiple times a day even, for us to stay aligned. It is the very place where God reveals Himself to us, His plans and His purpose for us in every situation is already written out there, we just need to seek it first and foremost, and with all our hearts. Surprisingly, the more time we spend meditating on His Word, the more it becomes our nature. Think about that for a moment. Through meditation on His word, His divine nature is not only revealed to us, but it can become a part of us, a part of our very own nature. What a gift!!

Furthermore, He sent his only begotten Son, Jesus Christ, to earth to help clarify His Word for us here as The Word Manifest. While Jesus was on earth, He *was* God Manifested on this planet. His Word was living, breathing, and dwelling among us:

That which was from the beginning, which we have heard, which we have seen with our eyes, which we have looked at and our hands have touched—this we proclaim concerning the Word of life. 1 John 1-2

Just imagine how magnificent it must have been to encounter His word in the flesh, to be one of His disciples in the time while He was here. Imagine getting the chance to actually follow Him in person while absorbing all of that divine Truth along the way! And although He is no longer with us here in the flesh, as God Manifest on earth, He did send us His Helper (the Holy Spirit) to help guide us as we live intentional lives of discipleship and follow Him. Thus, the importance and beauty of being active and awake in spirit *with His Spirit.*

God also speaks to us through His spoken word, known as "rhema". When we have received Christ as our savior and have welcomed His Holy Spirit into us, we can receive a "rhema" message from Him. By seeking His Word in the Scriptures to help guide us through a specific situation, He can utter His wisdom and discernment to us in our spirits, through His Holy Spirit. This often comes in the form of fresh revelation when we go over familiar verses. I know I get consistent delight out of verses that arise in my mind during specific situations. I will open my Bible, commentaries, and lexicon resources to search deeper in The Word about that verse, and then suddenly I find myself grasping something entirely new and relevant just when I need it most. Of course, it doesn't just happen passively to us, we have to actively seek His Word, study it, revel in it, and meditate on it. Then, it becomes the most valuable part of us as we digest it and internalize it.

The Spirit gives life; the flesh counts for nothing. The words I have spoken to you--they are full of the Spirit and life. John 6:63

His Word is more powerful than any other device, or weapon of the enemy that can be formed against us such as confusion, anxiety, turmoil, and unrest. His Word can literally divide the intentions of our soul from our spirit and make the intentions of our hearts clear. We should seek it in times where we feel we are lacking clarity, or when any type of chaos or confusion sets in:

"For the word of God is quick, and powerful, and sharper than any twoedged sword, piercing even to the dividing asunder of soul and spirit, and of the joints and marrow, and is a discerner of the thoughts and intents of the heart." Hebrews 4:12

Are You Ready To Live Awake?

All of this is only possible if and when we are spiritually awake in Christ. If that part of our beings, the spirit, is born again and no longer dead. If our body and soul has accepted Christ as our Savior, and the spirit is now actively communicating and engaging in communion with God, it has received the Holy Spirit. Without this, we are not truly capable of hearing God as He speaks to us. This is why I wrote "awaken" out as the very first step to aligning body, soul, and spirit in Faith, by Grace. Once we grasp this, it's easy to see how God could have easily been speaking to us all along, we just weren't willing to hear Him.

Willingness plays another big role in awakening our spirits to His spirit. If we aren't willing to bare our souls and get totally raw with ourselves and God, then we aren't truly willing to receive His Divine Alignment in our lives and beings. I clung for so long to my own strength and ability, that out of mere rebellion I refused to admit how weak I knew I had truly become. This became a classic tale of self-defeating prophecy of sabotage, where I'd fall into the same cycle of destruction time and time again, relentlessly refusing to admit the very real consequences I was facing. I'd bounce between awareness of these consequences, and then turning off my will to even care by numbing them out with substance abuse. Not everyone is so self-destructive, but if you are, or have been, I want you to know that I've been there, and you can come out of it!

Similarly, if we tread through life without having our God consciousness active, we are spiritually comatose. This is a life where we actually become complacent in remaining stagnant, or even worse, indifferent to knowing that we are constantly backsliding:

And that, knowing the time, that now it is high time to awake out of sleep: for now is our salvation nearer than when we believed. Romans 13:11

You might've already been wondering how I could have possibly been an upright yoga teacher, leading classes and even recognized as a pillar of health and wellness in a military community and still secretly struggling with drug and alcohol abuse. Well, I will be honest. I was incredibly good at living double-mindedly. On a good day, I'd rise in the morning and be fully present for what I had to conquer that day. I was consistent about showing up for the community as their peaceful and calm teacher who drank pressed fruit and veggie juices and ate fresh, and then by nighttime I'd unfold into what I can say was a very dark version of myself, either privately, or socially. South Beach, in Miami, Florida, was where I came to know yoga as my "healthy lifestyle alternative". It was often accompanied by late night clubbing, partying with substances that caused us to stay up until morning, sometimes even for several days at a time. I thought, if I could maintain this balance where I was "healthy by day" or at least most days, and then wildly destructive by night, somehow it might all balance out. Unfortunately, I was not alone in this thinking. A lot of other health and wellness pillars in that community, like fellow yoga teachers and fitness trainers, also took to lavish amounts of alcohol, smoking weed, and doing coke by day/night (among other things). This only furthered my deception that this could somehow be normal.

Maybe your experience has been less actively destructive, and more passively living and hoping for the best to manifest as you go about doing the "next best thing". Sadly, even our best intentions fail sometimes, which is why that age-old saying goes, "The road to hell is paved with good intentions". It took my crash and burn scenario to finally admit this to myself, to others, to God, and to finally relinquish my own will, my own desires, and my own "best intentions" over to Him. I was finally fully ready to receive His will, His divine purpose, and follow His plan for my life.

Perhaps, you were even less rebellious in your passivity. Maybe you're just longing for a clear and direct route to aligning His plan, purpose, and will for your life, and for whatever reason, you feel like maybe you are just going through life in a sleeplike state. I know for sure that I have felt this, and sometimes even still do when I find myself questioning if a certain project or next step is actually His will for me. I'll be the first to admit that when this type of doubt sets in, I have to fight the urge to succumb to slothlike living. It's kind of like just going through the motions, where you think you have figured out what works and know just how little you can get by with doing, or not doing? It's life on auto-pilot mode. Instead of allowing God to take the wheel and guide us along His divine purpose and Will for our lives, we just float passively by. During this time God may have been speaking to us, sending us signs, and trying to captivate us with His love, but we were asleep, so we weren't really trying to listen.

Life like this can become mundane pretty quickly, and that's when the real trouble sets in for me. I start seeking other distractions and pleasures to fill the void I've created by simply turning off my spiritual being. Are you starting to see the deadly cycle that I was referring to earlier? It's so real, and when we've lived long enough, with the right heart positioning, God can reveal these triggers in our own lives that we need to avoid and run to Him for our refuge and strength. I went through life like this, suffering through the cycles, for a pretty long time. At first, it started with a childlike rebellion against the way I was raised, which was in a Christian home with my father as a hardworking businessman, and also separately as a devoted pastor. I spent my childhood in church, and was encouraged to keep it up in my young adult life, but I chose rebellion instead. Eventually, I found myself purposefully refraining from any correction by others, or even myself, in my spirit. I let the spirit part of my being fall into a deep sleep. So when I eventually allowed myself to succumb to a life best lived in numbness, it wasn't a huge stepping stone for me to add dabbling in drugs and overly consuming alcohol from there. I did these things on purpose, to dull out the pain of my past and current situations that had become ever so evident after years of spiritual neglect. I somewhat quickly came to a place where I felt like I had no control over anything in my life, I'd just refused to admit it, or that I actually cared. The auto-pilot mode was all I knew how to do and I didn't even know where to begin if I did choose to care that day. This eventually led to full blown addictions that became yet another wall and barrier keeping me from spiritual awareness. Another thing I had to either conquer and heal, or continue to passively submit to and just continue to float on, hoping I would somehow keep getting by. I became so complacent in running from reality and feeling, that I ultimately found myself totally disconnected to both myself and the others around me who truly loved me. At a relatively young adult age, I had already forgotten who I was, and how to get back to my perception of my "true self". Now, instead of just seeking one aspect of healing, I needed more, I was lost in body, soul, and spirit, and I felt totally dead inside. If you are this far gone, don't worry, I was too, and there is good news yet to come!

Alive In Christ

The good news came when I finally surrendered my life back to Christ. I had hit rock bottom, as some would say, and I had to hit it more than once to finally admit I was there, and to finally surrender that rebellious spirit inside me that kept me fighting for no apparent reason to do life my own way. It was not until a completely public display of erratic behavior that led to divorce, and the subsequent utter abandonment of myself and my son in another part of the country by my former husband, for me to say, "I can't continue on this way, God, save me!" I am just so grateful that deep down, I still knew that there was a way. Deep down, because of how I was diligently raised up in the church, I always knew that Jesus Christ was the only way. Thank God He kept me alive for as long as He did, to give me another chance to finally turn back and say "I'm yours God, I'm all yours!" and give me a chance to live life fully alive in Christ!

Let's walk through a passage together that I found fresh revelation in after going through these self-realizations, and I hope you will too. It is called "*By Grace Through Faith*" and can be found in *Ephesians 2 verses 1-10 (NKJV)*:

[1] And you He made alive, who were dead in your trespasses and sins, [2] in which you once walked according to the course of this world, according to the prince of the power of the

air, the spirit who now works in the sons of disobedience, [3] among whom also we all once conducted ourselves in the lusts of our flesh, fulfilling the desires of the flesh and of the mind, and were by nature children of wrath, just as the others.

Let's pause here. In verse 1, it confirms exactly how I was feeling: I felt dead because I was dead, in my trespasses and in my sins. I was furious with rebellion and a somewhat proud daughter of disobedience. By fulfilling the curiosities of my own fleshly desires and will, I found myself totally lost, amongst the others who were also lost in the world. Perhaps you can relate? Continuing on...

[4] But God, who is rich in mercy, because of His great love with which he loved us, [5] even when we were dead in trespasses, made us alive together with Christ (by grace you have been saved), [6] and raised us up together, and made us sit together in the heavenly places in Christ Jesus,

Take a moment to wonder in awe at the infinite mercy and love that God must have for each and every one of His children, even when we were acting as sons and daughters of disobedience, dead in our sins. This just confirms that there is no perfect time to turn to God other than right now. There is no prerequisite to achieve, and no state of cleansing ourselves that we could possibly complete that would ever make us pure enough to be worthy of His love and mercy, yet He gives it freely through His son Jesus Christ who holds a high seat in heaven. Even more, He fulfills the promise that He has already raised us up together with Jesus. Just imagine that! There is a royal table in the heavenly places with a seat next to Jesus with your name on it. That whole "you can't sit with us" meme that became popular in social media hardly places in comparison to having a seat next to the One and Only Savior!

[7] that in the ages to come He might show the exceeding riches of His grace in His kindness towards us in Christ Jesus.

The promise of His infinite mercy and grace is just that, infinite. It was, and is, and is to come, and we are able to receive it through Jesus Christ.

[8] For by grace you have been saved through faith, and that not of yourself; it is the gift of God, [9] not of works, lest anyone should boast.

We can't earn our way into heaven; we would never possibly be able to! It is by His infinite grace, mercy, forgiveness and love that we were given His son Jesus Christ as redeemer of our souls. When we confess with our hearts and mouths that we believe this, then we receive the most glorious gift of God, our salvation!

[10] For we are His workmanship, created in Christ Jesus for good works, which God prepared beforehand that we should walk in them.

So God prepared His divine plan and purpose for you before you even came to exist. He created you in His image, as His workmanship, and through the acceptance and willful following of Christ Jesus, we can achieve good works that lead us in the right path, His path.

After my spiritual awakening, and consciously reconnecting my spirit with His spirit, I began to truly accept His call on my life, as one of His chosen ones. This became my inspiration, my motivation, and my new identity.

"For many are called, but few are chosen." Matthew 22:14

In this short but very sweet verse, Jesus summarizes an entire parable. It takes place in a wedding scene, and correlates to being one of God's "chosen ones". He explains that there are many who receive an invite, and that there is more than one way to respond to an invitation. Some will answer by saying "yes", and others will politely decline. Even so, others will not so politely decline and take it as an opportunity to offend the invitee, and then there are those who will totally ignore it, with no response whatsoever. If you've ever planned a large event or a wedding, perhaps you may have experienced this type of scenario. I actually experienced all of those when planning my wedding to Joe, my husband. We had people excited to join, we had people lash out at us over past hurts and offend us, we had people politely decline, and we had people totally ignore the invite altogether. The external call that Jesus is referring to here is the invitation that His Father has sent out to all people: For repentance and faith. It is a message He sent to us all very clearly through His Son Jesus Christ, echoed by His disciples, and very consistent in His Word. It is the receiving of the internal call that is the key to becoming one of The Chosen. If you receive the internal call, you are actively choosing to surrender your own plans and will, and choosing to accept the faith with repentance. This is how you truly RSVP "Yes" to the call, and receive His Spirit along with the redeeming grace of eternal life and salvation.

"But to those called by God to salvation, both Jews and Gentiles, Christ is the power of God and the wisdom of God. 1 Corinthians 1:24

You could also think about it like a phone call. In our daily lives we probably receive lots of calls, and if you're like me, you screen those calls. Imagine one that comes in and says "repent to faith" across the screen. You might be like "Woah, let me just send this to voicemail, that sounds scary, and like a lot of work". Or maybe you hit decline all together, or even "block this caller". Well, God is patient, and God is love, so if He has chosen you, He won't give up that easily on His calls to you. However, it is no light gesture to slight the King of the Universe and all of creation. I know that He was very patient with me through my rebellious phase that lasted over a decade. I am so grateful I did not meet Him on Judgement Day prior to finally surrendering to answer that Call, and that He kept on calling me, relentlessly. It truly was my own stubborn heart that refused to accept it, and for that I have deeply repented.

So as you can see, it all begins with admitting to yourself and to God that we need Him to help us become spiritually aware, and that we are ready to take on this process. It's like an internal awakening of our soul with His Spirit.

New Life in Christ, Ephesians 4:17-24

So I tell you this, and insist on it in the Lord, that you must no longer walk as the Gentiles do, in the futility of their thinking. They are darkened in their understanding and alienated from the life of God because of the ignorance that is in them due to the hardness of their hearts. Having lost all sense of shame, they have given themselves over to sensuality for the practice of every kind of impurity, with a craving for more.

But this is not the way you came to know Christ. Surely you heard of Him and were taught in Him—in keeping with the truth that is in Jesus— to put off your former way of life, your old self, which is being corrupted by its deceitful desires; to be renewed in the spirit of your minds; and to put on the new self, created to be like God in true righteousness and holiness.

It takes a bold amount of honesty and transparency for us to be willing to put off our former way of life and let Him totally in. If you haven't committed to answering His call yet, and are ready, then take a moment to prepare your heart and quiet your mind as you say this prayer out loud:

"Heavenly Father, I come before you now, just as I am. Lord, I know you have pursued me and that you have seen me. I know that you love me, even in my shortcomings. I surrender myself to Your Will. I give you my whole heart, and my whole self, I surrender to you. Take my body, soul, and spirit and make me new. Make me a new creation in You. Forgive me of my sins, and help me to forgive others who have sinned against me. Help me to see the places I need change in my life, and give me the will and strength to do it. Thank You for Your saving grace Father, and your infinite mercy. Thank You for the sweet gift of Salvation through Your son Christ Jesus, My King. Thank you for loving me so much that you sent your only Son to die for my sins, and to rise again in His glorious resurrection. Thank You for choosing me to be Your child, one of Your chosen ones, and help me to do Your work with the rest of my time here on earth. In Jesus Name I pray, Amen."

Whew. That's a hefty load off the shoulders, am I right? It just feels so good to say those words out loud, and repeat them whenever you need to feel that loftiness in heart and spirit. He delights when we come to Him, and sometimes we need a renewing of spirit in tough times. There's no shame in offering up prayer. We will indeed encounter trials, tribulations and temptations in our walks here on earth, but if we are truly committed to following His Way in our hearts as we seek Him, He will reveal His will for us, and give us the strength to overcome what we face. We may be pleasantly surprised by the good that He reveals in us, a fresh perspective that perhaps many of us have not seen in our own elves for some time. Of course, we must also be prepared for Him to reveal the ugly and the nastiness that we might have inside, with the courage and faith that what He brings us to, He will bring us through.

Walking With The Spirit (Conviction)

Search me, God, and know my heart; test me and know my anxious thoughts. See if there is any offensive way in me, and lead me in the way everlasting. Psalms 139:23-24

It can start with a simple prayer like this Psalm, where we invite the Holy Spirit to reveal the areas we may need His correction and direction in. In other words, we can begin praying for conviction by His Holy Spirit within our own spirits. We ask Him to show us what to strip away, what to keep, and how to live more purely in the eyes of the Lord. This is how we invite the Holy Spirit to begin His transformational work in making us a new creation in Him. When you ask The Lord to test you and show you your anxious thoughts, He will act! In these times, be watchful for how He moves in you and around you, and be prepared for the tests that might arise. Try to greet them as opportunities that are opening your eyes and heart. Take this opportunity to shift your instincts and reactions to God-conscious actions. You can do this by pausing once you identify a "test" or trial. This can come as an uncomfortable feeling or experience, or a temptation, or a "trigger" that would normally incite a gut reaction from you instinctively that you know is probably "wrong", but you often don't think twice about moving forward with. These are the moments we have to yield to the conviction of the Holy Spirit by saying "Thank you for showing me this shift in my spirit, and now give me the strength to seek and do Your will here. Not by my might, but by the Spirit's!" He will show up for you if you call on Him and you rely on Him. It's a supernatural strength that comes from the heart positioning of our own honest willingness, and the full reliance and trust in our faith in the Lord and His power and ability to make us overcomers in any situation.

I've gone through seasons where I've recognized a major shift was needed in my life. In those times, I get into the habit of saying this prayer in Psalms 139: 23-24 often. I'll be honest: I know that when I do, I'm in for a proper lesson. I even said it one morning, kind of nonchalantly while driving to a doctor's appointment, and would you believe that as I walked in and wrote my name down on the sign-in sheet, I noticed the waiting room was four times as full as I had ever seen it? This doctor was notorious for making patients wait up to two hours on a regular day; and with this many people ahead of me I knew I was in for it. I had purposefully chosen the first available appointment time in the morning and arranged for my mother to watch our toddler while our teen son was at football practice, all so I could be in and out as quickly as possible. I had worked really hard and had to rely on others to help so that I could be done in time to pick up the teen from practice, and cook lunch, and relieve my mother from babysitting. It was also a visit for our rainbow baby, the miracle of life that arrives after a miscarriage. You can imagine that these visits to the doctor carried their own special weight of anxiousness. Instead of getting angry about my time, and the graciousness of my mother's time for helping me to be there being totally wasted; or letting worry flash through my mind as it often tried to do in that delicate pregnancy: I paused and settled inward, with Him.

Taking deep breaths, I forced a smile onto my face. I knew that He was listening and that when we call on Him to test us and show us our anxious thoughts or shortcomings, even uncomfortably, that we can count on Him to reveal them. At the very same time, we can (and should) run to Him. That's when the genuine smile set in. Knowing we can throw ourselves into His arms with whatever unpleasantness that is revealed, that we can surrender it over to Him, is accompanied with such a sweet peace that it surpasses all understanding.

It's these types of awakenings where the growth comes, and the heart opens up, and The Spirit settles into the places we willingly remove our own "selves" from occupying. It's healing and renewal all in one stroke, *if* we are aware and awake in The Spirit as it happens around us, and in us.

For any of this to take place, we require a truly *humble heart posture*. Even better: *A servant's heart*. When we are willing to humbly lay our own selves aside, our own thoughts, agendas, and pride, we create fresh space inside us. With a servant's heart we can give this space over to Him.

"Lord, create in me a pure heart and renew a steadfast spirit within me". Psalms 51:10

As we go through life using this approach, it becomes a daily (or multiple times per day) routine. Constantly opening ourselves up to His Spirit and inviting Him to occupy our body, soul, and spirit. We can then make a habit out of acknowledging these convictions in prayer and confession, all the while knowing and trusting that He is for us.

"And we know that in all things God works for the good of those who love him, who have been called according to his purpose." Romans 8:28

This verse has brought tremendous comfort to me in times where my thoughts and understandings were limited. In times where I could not see a reason why God would allow bad things to happen to me even though I was seeking Him fully and following a trajectory I was certain He had led me to. This was also my grandmother's most favorite verse. When our cousin, her nephew, passed away in a tragic car accident at the young age of 16, these were the first words out of her mouth when she heard the news. Imagine the type of Faith, the type of Love for God that must possess your heart in order for you to turn, even at a time of utter despair, to Him in full trust with the knowledge that whatever happens, or has happened, He has already prepared The Way for you. To trust fully and even blindly sometimes, that He is for you. It means that life will not always be comfortable, that we will go through the highs and lows, but if we have Him within us, and we are walking with Him, He will carry us through it.

This first step towards alignment brings us to a place where we become willing and prepared to be refined by His Fire. It's where the conscious daily effort of His purification begins, and how we become transformed, and it often comes through the trials and tribulations of life.

2 TRANSFORM

Therefore, if anyone is in Christ, he is a new creation; old things have passed away; behold, all things have become new. 2 Corinthians 5:17

They don't call it a refining fire for no good reason. Upon Salvation and accepting eternal life in Christ, we are still left to live our days on this sin trodden earth, only now as the Chosen ones and beacons of His light. For most of us, properly letting go of our old identities takes a shedding of our old routines and behaviors. As we've discussed, this requires repenting, renouncing, and most of all, a real commitment to change. At first, it can feel pretty massive, and even overwhelming, but don't let the enemy taunt you into believing you can't do it. You are not alone, and you don't have to rely solely on your own rational thought, self-control, or personal will. No, our transformation is one-hundred percent a co-creative process and it involves your body, soul, spirit, *and Christ*. Furthermore, God doesn't require us to be totally sinless when we come to Him, and a good thing at that because all of us would one-hundred percent fail if we tried. He wants us now, just as we are, and He will help us clean up our lives through His Son Christ who covered all of our sins. We could never earn the righteousness of Christ, and we would never be able to remove all sin from our lives, but that shouldn't stop us from laying it all down at His feet and putting our best foot forward to begin walking as His beloved child each and every day, in His will for us.

Surrendering To His Will

For God made Christ, who never sinned, to be the offering for our sin, so that we could be made right with God through Christ. 2 Corinthians 5:21

When it finally dawned on me that I was called, that I was one of His Chosen to live with a higher purpose (His purpose), and that I was truly a daughter of The King, I received the conviction of the Holy Spirit to make real and sincere changes in my lifestyle. A whole season of repentance followed after this for me. I'm not talking just little things at a time; I'm talking about being intentional and completely shifting from my former self and ways. I felt convicted to become more modest in the way I dressed, I had to change my daily routines like practicing worldly meditations and checking my horoscope, I needed to leave my career as a yoga teacher, quit binge drinking (and other abusive behaviors), stop cursing and listening to profane music, remove icons of false gods (buddhas and Sanskrit singing bowls I'd acquired from yoga), destroy the altar I had created in my yoga studio, stop sacrificing myself to others for the sake of seeking "love" and "acceptance", and the list goes on. See, when I finally truly saw myself after my spiritual awakening through Christ, I realized I had a lot that was severely broken. I realized that I needed Him to put me back together in a new way. It was a total and necessary transformation, and it was only possible because He helped me through, every step of the way. He can and will do this for you too!

A lovely little book I picked up along the way really helped me to see this whole repentance, transformation and conviction phase in a desirable light. It is called *The Christian's Secret of a Happy Life*. In it, Hannah Whitall Smith paints a perfect picture of our beings having both emotion and will. Our emotions are products of our flesh. They are at the whims of our senses, and they can flux as high and low as the tides at any given onset of sensory perception. When we feel pain, discomfort, or unease, we can allow our emotions to reign as king of our bodies and minds, and they can lead us to do some truly horrific things. For one, this is how I picked up some of my worst habits, like binge drinking, smoking and drug abuse. Whenever my emotions would run wild, I'd use them as a qualified excuse to necessarily abuse these substances and numb out my feelings and emotions. It was a terrible cycle, and one that almost killed me more than once.

Emotions can be wildly crazy and unsteady; we have all been there and

19

experienced both highs and lows. Just because emotions can be incredibly strong, it doesn't mean that we should let them run, or ruin, our lives.

On page 77, Smith says: "Our emotions belong to us, and are suffered and enjoyed by us, but they are not ourselves; and if God is to take possession of us, it must be into this central will or personality that He enters. If, then, He is reigning there by the power of His Spirit, all the rest of our nature must come under His sway; and as the will is, so is the man."

Opposition sets in when our emotions go in one direction, our will in another, and what we know and believe God's will to be in yet another direction. This is why we must make a conscious and intentional surrendering of our entire will, over to Him. It may be easier said than done at first, but with sincere commitment, the yoke is truly easy, and the burden is truly light, just as He promised us in His Word. Much lighter and easier than doing things "our way". A phrase that is well known from The Lord's Prayer, "Thy will be done!", is an excellent verse to train your mind with by repeating it when you find your emotions rearing up and your will being taunted. Mutter it as you surrender your ego and yourself back unto Him.

On page 79 Smith reveals "the secret":

She says, "The secret lies just here- that our will, which is the spring of all our actions, has been in the past under the control of sin and self, and these have worked in us all for their own good pleasure. But now God calls upon us to yield our wills up unto Him, and that He may take the control of them, and may work in us to will and to do of His good pleasure. If we will obey this call and present ourselves to Him as a living sacrifice, He will take possession of our surrendered wills, and will begin at once to work in us "that which is well pleasing in His sight, through Jesus Christ," giving us the mind that was in Christ, and transforming us into His image."

The goal here is to reach a point where our emotions actually rejoice in His will. That when we look in the mirror, we can be proud to present ourselves to Him as a living sacrifice. Our bodies, pure and clean temples unto Him, and not just our higher selves (like my former yoga practice had me believing). I think this was the real turning point for me. My heart and soul repositioned and I found my desires and wills *wanting to please God*. I longed to hear Him say, *"This is my daughter, with whom I am pleased"*. There was no longer any part of me lingering in the dark, trying to hide the sinful actions I had truly come to love in my decrepit self-nature, from Him. I had to lay my entire being, my emotions and will, all laid down at His Feet.

What also really made the transformation of living with His will versus my own as a priority was knowing and trusting that I could come just as I was. That there was no prerequisite training or cleansing of my sins that I could do other than what I had already done, which was truly accepting Christ as my Savior and committing my will over to Him. When we show up to God, baring our hearts and souls to Him with all the nastiness we have done and brokenness we carry inside, He does not greet us in anger. In fact, He delights to show us mercy!

Who is a God like you, who pardons sin and forgives the transgression of the remnant of his inheritance? You do not stay angry forever but delight to show mercy. Micah 7:18

Why would we even try to run and hide from such a loving God, whom we know is both infinite and intimate?

Repent

A gorgeous transformation has begun to take place as we learn to hear God, to walk with His Spirit, receive His conviction, while also actively surrendering our own will to Him. It is now, where we are ready to see the fruits of surrendering to His grace, by repenting. I honestly found the word "repentance" to be quite scary until I tried it myself. It sounded awful to me because it conjured up notions of medieval catholic England and a Papal pardon costing my month's wages, or even a self-inflicted painful punishment, like lashings. It was hardly something I would equate with the "fruits of His grace", but that is because I had no idea what true repentance was before sincerely embarking on my journey of realignment in faith, or how sweet and liberating it was to lay myself down in utter surrender to His grace.

Now, it is in repentance that I find myself intimately close to God. There is something divinely pure about the essence of coming clean in front of Him. It's not something I do once and awhile, rather I have a habit now of repenting often, even daily. It's not a ritual, and it doesn't have to be a long drawn-out conversation with Him either, although some days are just like that. I like to get down on my knees when I repent to God, sometimes I'm even bent over with my face down on the floor, and I literally let it all out here. I let it flow out of me, the wrongs I've done, the hurt I've been carrying, the sin I know I grew to love out of my crooked nature that I want Him to change. Basically, I get clean before The Lord by airing all of my own dirty laundry out without holding anything back. It's almost immediately liberating just to get it all out, and then I give it directly over to Him: I put my whole life, my will, and all those horrible things I've done or thought of, and I give them over to Him. I trust Him and promise to obey Him, as I know He will show me the way to grow beyond these things, if I just continue to listen to Him, to walk with His Spirit, and surrender to His grace.

Think about this: With every breath we give an offering, for He gave everything He is for what we are not, and could never be. God is so powerful, and He is so personal. When we give Him all of our love, our heart and soul, He forgives and He does not hold our sins of the past over us forever. He delights in steadfast love. He truly does not want to stay in a position of anger against us, and even His anger is a form of love.

Perhaps you know this type of love. It is like when a child disobeys a command a parent has given, either intentionally or unintentionally. The parent might react first with anger, voicing correction, and perhaps even discipline, but then comes compassion, because the child is loved wholly. See, The Lord is the Master Creator of Agape, the type of unconditional love that only He can truly give. We aspire to show unconditional love to our loved ones, but surely none of us can be just like God. Imagine how quick He is to show us this compassion, heal us, and help us transform into the new creation that He promises we can be in Him. For this reason, I believe the immediate step following repentance, and committing to renouncing our old ways, is praise!

Praise Him

Our greatest comfort will always come from praising Him. When heaviness creeps in, and it often does when we spiritually awaken and start to become actively aware of new depths in our beings, we must cloak ourselves in the garment of His praise. When sadness appears in the ashes of our past, we can pour the oil of joy upon it as we glorify His name. It might seem counterintuitive, but it's been written and promised, and in my experience, it truly works:

To appoint unto them that mourn in Zion, to give unto them beauty for ashes, the oil of joy for mourning, the garment of praise for the spirit of heaviness, that they might be called trees of righteousness, the planting of the Lord, that He might be glorified. Isaiah 61:3

We must embrace our new identity as we struggle with our old tendencies, rejoicing that God has given us the freedom from our bondage to sin, and the power to continually overcome it in Him.

"With God all things are possible" (Matthew 19:26), especially when it seems impossible to us.

Abiding in Him as a lifestyle means we will face a daily struggle with our flesh, and I've dedicated a whole chapter to this later on in the book. After all, we live in a fallen world where God is still sovereign, but sin abounds with Satan as the "prince of the power of the air" (Ephesians 2:2) and "ruler of this world" (John 12:31). However, we do not have this bondage to sin the same way that unbelievers do, and thus we are given an upper hand in aligning our minds with the truest form of love for self and others.

His Love + Light

We must focus our energy on giving and receiving the love and light of Christ.

The god of this age has blinded the minds of unbelievers, so that they cannot see the light of the gospel that displays the glory of Christ, who is the image of God.

2 Corinthians 4:4

Recalling from Genesis that God created man in His image, we can be certain that emanating the light of the gospel that displays the glory of Christ is our best identity. This is why, as we grow stronger and bolder in our God-given identity, we are able

to truly love ourselves, our neighbors, and even our enemies.

"But I say to you, love your enemies, bless those who curse you, do good to those who hate you, and pray for those who spitefully use you and persecute you." Matthew 5:44

The deeper our relationship grows with Christ, the more aligned our body, soul, and spirit becomes with Him, and the greater we can shine His light. Once we get a glimpse of this transformation and new creation, it's important to understand that it is always changing and growing, from glory to glory.

"But we all, with unveiled face, beholding as in a mirror the glory of the Lord, are being transformed into the same image from glory to glory, just as by the Spirit of the Lord." 2 Corinthians 3:18

We know that we will have daily battles against our flesh and that the enemy will try to come in with trials, tests, and tribulations. When feelings of former or current sin, guilt and shame arise, it's important to deal with them by surrendering them over to Christ with true repentance and a commitment to renunciation. By repenting and renouncing the habits and tendencies of our former self, we continue to transform our new creation in Him. Even the Apostle Paul admitted to having to practice this every single day when he said, "I die daily".

Here is where we debunk a great myth that has seemingly taken over and replaced The Truth in recent days:

Many self-help books and coaches are teaching us that we have to love ourselves first and foremost, and that out of self-love stems all the abilities and possibilities for opportunity in our life. Without self-love, they tell us we cannot truly love another, or seize what is out there teeming in the "infinite vastness the universe is holding just for us" ...

Okay, now it's time to be clear: We should love ourselves, but there is a transformation to this type of love that is key to doing it right, and it comes along with the transformation of our new creations:

Then Jesus told his disciples, "If anyone would come after me, let him deny himself and take up his cross and follow me. For whoever would save his life will lose it, but whoever loses his life for my sake will find it. Matthew 16: 24-25

If we are holding onto our old "selves", and our old selfish ways of doing things, we might not be getting this whole self-love thing right. Is it important to take care of yourself, putting your health and self-care as a priority? Of course. But, it's very clear that if we are trying to love and honor ourselves and the flesh instead of putting God first, we may have this self-love equation backwards:

"But seek first the kingdom of God and his righteousness, and all these things will be added to you." Matthew 6:33

God's greatest commandment is to love Him first, and if we do, He promises to give us all that we need:

"And he said to him, "You shall love the Lord your God with all your heart and with all your soul and with all your mind. This is the great and first commandment."
Matthew 22:37-38

If we dive deeper into the meaning of the original Greek words used in this verse, we can find a valuable tool, a most essential tool, on how to love:

The Greek word used here for soul is "psuche", and it implies "our mind, our will, our emotions, our personality, and desires" in the same context as we discussed in Step 1 for 1 Thessalonians 5:23. The Greek word for the mind that is being used in this verse is "dianoia". It is a feminine noun that means "the mind, disposition, or thought"; and originates from the Greek preposition "dia", meaning "through, on account of, or because of", and the verb "noéo", to think, or perceive.

So, the purpose of these words being used here in this verse is to encourage us to intensify our thoughts. When our will, emotions, desires, or personality creeps in, rather than letting them run wild by ruling our actions and words, we are to emphasize critical thinking. With thorough reasoning, we consider both sides of the matter. When our will and flesh rears up and wants to battle against what I like to call our "God conscience" (what we feel deep down is probably against His Will and His word), we must apply this tool of higher reasoning by seeking Him to intercede as we reach a balanced conclusion. It is totally helpful when we come across personal triggers in life, and has surely saved me from falling down a rabbit hole of darkness more than once as my perceived emotions and wills had often previously done.

This is the type of action in the mind that is essential to fully loving God, ourselves, and others. It is more than a type of action; it is a tool and an instrument that we are called to greatly practice. However, it is not of our own self-control or will that we are to apply it. When it is practiced without

God's light, it can be incredibly self-destructive:

"He has performed mighty deeds with His arm; He has scattered those who are proud in the thoughts of their hearts." Luke 1:51

So, self-love is actually supposed to look like loving the self-less, honoring our own wills and desires less, and loving God and His more. It is a selfless and sacrificial love we gain by losing our "self" to Him. Only then will we experience true love, a deeper intimacy than any type of surface love the flesh could possibly offer.

Love God First

Loving God first is also the key to loving first, and our transformation into new creations. Afterall, God is love. When we put Him first, we are also putting love first in all aspects, and we will go over this in depth in Step 7 where we explore the crucial step of Loving One Another.

It suddenly becomes obvious and evident why having a deep-rooted love and connection with God The Father, His Son Jesus Christ, and The Holy Spirit is vitally important *before* any type of "love of self". If we love God first, and not ourselves, then we will learn to see ourselves how He sees us. We will know that we are who He says we are, and will ultimately fall in a deep and solid love with that very best most beautiful version of ourselves. It's not about the superficial layers, where self-love practices often rest, like "I accept myself wholly for my body image, or my shortcomings, or my weaknesses" In fact, we come to a place where we are okay knowing we are not worthy of the infinite love, mercy, and grace that God gives us *despite our weakness and shortcomings.* In fact, it is a lot less like God loving us for how great we think we are or are trying to become, and a lot more like God loving us *despite ourselves* that spurs such gratitude in our souls. It's deep within our spirits and in our souls that we start the healing when we work in and through God's love for us.

Ultimately, this whole practice of self-love, when done in God's love, culminates into the transformation of our very identities. It becomes how we view ourselves, how others view us, and what our true purpose is in His will and perfect plan for us. Thankfully, as believers, we know that our best identity can only be found in Christ. The more we walk with Him, the more we will be able to see who He created us to truly be; and the more we endure with a steadfast spirit, the more clearly we will see what we need to nurture as we continue to transform, and what we need to let go of.

His Perfect Plan For You

Two places that I often go to in The Word when I am seeking reaffirmation of His ability to wholly transform me from the inside out and lead me to my predestined purpose in His will are found in Psalms and in the book of Jeremiah.

"Create in me a pure heart and renew a steadfast spirit in me". Psalm 51:10

"For I know the plans I have for you," declares the Lord, "plans to prosper you and not to harm you, plans to give you hope and a future. Then you will call on me and come and pray to me, and I will listen to you. You will seek me and find me when you seek me with all your heart. I will be found by you," declares the Lord, "and will bring you back from captivity. I will gather you from all the nations and places where I have banished you," declares the Lord, "and will bring you back to the place from which I carried you into exile." Jeremiah 29:11-14

3 HEAL

Beginning with the body:

As we go through major transformations, we notice that there are many layers involved in change. At this point in the process, we might even start to feel vulnerable as we shift from our deepest inward being and point our body, soul, and spirit towards Christ. One thing we know for certain is we cannot rush the healing process. The care and management of our bodies, and making physical changes such as new behaviors, breaking old bad habits, and setting new spiritually healthy patterns for ourselves may be most obvious, although these may not necessarily come with ease every day. Thankfully, we can monitor them outwardly, as they deal with the senses of sight, hearing, smelling, feeling, touching, tasting, and etc.

Make Healing Changes

I was once a smoker, a really habitual smoker, and after I received the conviction by the Holy Spirit to live for Christ, I started seeing that as a burnt offering of literal trash. In the Old Testament, people used to offer burnt offerings that were to be sweet aromas to God, to conjure His presence with them. Now, we know we don't need to do that anymore because Jesus came to fulfill the old law, and that once we become one spirit united with His Holy Spirit, His presence is with us whenever we seek Him. So, if I'm one with His spirit, then when I'm smoking, I'm basically sitting there blowing toxic smoke in His face. This realization suddenly helped me become completely disgusted by the act, and over a period of just a couple weeks, I managed to fully quit.

The same happened when it came to binge drinking, and drugs, which I used to do far too often. I had used a lot of excuses to justify why this had become a bad habit of mine, but those twisted emotions only helped me validate the behavior with irrational reasoning. Once I let my God conscience in, and invited His Will to overtake mine, the way I perceived myself began to transform. I went from seeing myself, my broken self that used all the brokenness to justify drinking and using substances into oblivion, to seeing myself the way He saw me. Suddenly, there was beauty amongst the ashes of what He was burning away from me, of my old life and old behaviors. I wanted more of that, and less of what I had previously clung to. I also prayed and asked Him to take the temptation away whenever I began to feel powerless, as it was in those low moments that I would usually surrender over my will, and submit myself wholly to the alcohol and drugs.

I know, because I have experienced it, that if we pray for the Fruit of The Spirit of self-control, and for wisdom and discernment to truly see what we need to heal from, and subsequently, what we need to let go of, that He will intervene. He will become our strength, our will, and He will do His part as Our Savior. He will heal us from the deepest darkest inner parts of our beings, to the outward shining rays of His light that we are called to be as His disciples.

Beware Of Counterfeit Christ Traps

Another major shift I had to take that involved my body was my ritual practice of yoga. In fact, it was more than just a practice and cutting out something I occasionally did, I had to leave my whole career as a yoga teacher. See, sometimes things can manifest as seemingly "good" on the surface, and that perception lasts just long enough to get you hooked. Before you know it, you're replacing what Christ could and should be doing through you and with you, with a counterfeit experience.

For me, I knew what had attracted me to this "world of yoga" was the lure of promised peace and calm for my body and mind. I was convinced that I was pursuing a life of wellness for my body and mind when I started practicing it. I also really enjoyed the inclusive community, the flexibility of classes, and availability in studios. They just seemed to have classes whenever I needed them, and wherever I seemed to go I met these really kind and peaceful yogis. The humility in most of the members, and the additional health benefits like increased flexibility and oxygen flow for my body all seemed like perks. What I didn't fully know, or care to acknowledge, was that I was opening myself, and my soul, up to a world of counterfeit Christ, not to mention inviting some destructively dangerous spirits into my life.

When I was seeking peace and calm, I ended up looking for a yoga class to fit in my schedule that day instead of spending time in The Word. Whenever I was in a new town, instead of looking for the body of Christ to connect with, I was building relationships in the yoga community. When my mind became flustered, I'd seek stillness in worldly meditation by emptying my thoughts, instead of meditating and being still in The Word. Ultimately, instead of practicing Christianity, I got really busy practicing being a "yogini".

Did I lead with humility and a servant's heart? I sure thought so when I was in the midst of it, but one major lesson I have learned since, is the dangers of false humility. You might know false humility if you have ever felt like you yourself needed to subjugate in the eyes of God. When you tell someone, "Oh no don't pray for me, I'm good, how can I pray for you?" None of us are perfect, and we all could use some prayer. When God hears these types of things, He probably rolls His eyes and says, this one thinks they are in control...

As my love and dedication for yoga progressed into teaching, the further I got away from Christ, and led others astray too. I actually was in control of an entire classroom of people who not only moved exactly how I told them to, when I told them to, but I also cued their breathing, and their thoughts. I'd chant with them and lead them literally through a body and "mind" practice that would be flushed with mantras and thoughts to ponder for the day, never leading them in the Word of God. Interesting side note: Did you know the word mantra is Sanskirt, and combines two root words: "mana", meaning mind/to think, and "tra", which means vehicle? This is heavily influential at the deepest level.

31

You might say that you have been to a yoga class that wasn't so "ritualistic" at your local gym, and I would say, that's great... but yoga IS yoga. It comprises a slew of subtle spiritual practices that many don't even realize they are doing when first introduced to them, such as: worldly mantras, meditations, and poses that exalt false Gods *and demons*. These are all the very essence of this practice, and that essence is absolutely spiritual. In fact, the spiritual facet is the whole point of the practice according to some of its founding members.

The Truth About Yoga

Since so many people are told that yoga can be exclusive of the "spiritual" part of practice, and not involve religion, I think it's important to explain a few things here to debunk these myths, lest you fall into the same traps along your healing journey that I did and become farther away from Christ rather than drawing near: The origin and the name of the word "yoga" dates back to roughly 5,000 years ago and comes from the sanskrit roots "yujir" and "yuj", literally meaning to yoke, to unite or join, to add. It's very first mention is in the Rig Veda, an ancient and sacred text used by the Brahmans, or Vedic Priests. The Veda used the word 'yoga' with the meaning of 'yoking', 'joining', 'coming together' and 'connection'. These Vedic priests were considered mystic seers, and they documented their beliefs in a collection of hundreds of scriptures called The Upanishads, culminating in the Bhagavad-Gîtâ around 500 B.C.E. This collection of works then went on to become the very foundations for Hinduism, and for the practice of Yoga.

Now, many will argue that over time, and most especially in the Western World, Yoga has lost this yoke, or connection, to the religion. Some are fervently seeking to reunite it, like Sheetah Shal, an official with the Hindu American Foundation. Her group seeks to provide what it calls "a progressive voice for American Hindus," and in 2017 they mounted a "take back yoga" campaign, including appearances at conferences and attempts to raise media awareness of the practice's Hindu origins.

B.K.S. Iyengar (one of the foremost yoga teachers in the world and founder of Iyengar Yoga) wrote about it quite succinctly in the preface to his book,

"The Illustrated Light on Yoga" by stating:

"Yoga is a timeless pragmatic science evolved over thousands of years dealing with the physical, moral, mental and spiritual well-being of man as a whole.

The Western reader may be surprised at the recurring reference to the Universal Spirit, to mythology and even some philosophical and moral principles. He must not forget that in ancient times all the higher achievements of man, and knowledge, art and power, were part of religion and were seen to belong to God and to His priestly servants on Earth. The Catholic Pope is the last such embodiment of divine knowledge and Power in the West. But formerly, even in the Western World, music, painting, architecture, philosophy and medicine, as well as wars, were always in the service of God. It is only very recently in India that these Arts and Sciences have begun to shake off the Divine - but with due respect, for the emancipation of man's will, as distinct from Divine will, we in India continue to value the purity of purpose, the humility of discipline and the selflessness that are the legacy of our long bondage to God. I consider it important as well as interesting that the reader should know the origin of asanas, and I have, therefore, included legends handed down by practicing Yogi's and Sages."

So, I ask you, is it still possible to practice yoga but not submit to this "yoke" or "connection", which is the very name and essence of this ancient "science", "art", "ritual", "practice" or whatever name chosen to describe it.

Does it not beg the very question as to what you are yoking to at the very least? If the answer is ambiguous does that not alone urk your very soul?

The answer seen most often to this question is that you are connecting to whatever personal belief, power, or God you have. Clearly, Iyengar had different feelings as mentioned above. So, if it is the Universal Spirit, or Allah, or Jesus, or maybe if you're an Atheist it's personalized to be Your Supreme Self, or Your Supreme Power.

Furthermore, the very nature of a practice is to make it become a ritual, so routine that it is automatic. Perhaps that sounds like offering ourselves wholly to something, opening our body, our minds, our hearts, our souls, and our spirits. Perhaps that sounds like commiting to serve something. Perhaps that means becoming a slave.

33

Notice Iyengar's direct usage of the term "bondage to God", and understanding that "yoga" means to connect or to yoke, and a bondslave, or a bondservant, is one that makes a long lasting and permanent commitment as a slave. In the Book of James 2, we see James The Just use the Greek word for bondservant, "*doulos*" to describe his relationship to Jesus. While this may have been a gesture of humility coming from the very brother of Jesus himself, I am sure there is no humility in shrugging off the clear and defined yoke and connection to any other God, or actively practicing a bondage to a God other than the One and Holy God of Israel.

The Word gives us clear direction in so many verses on this, but here are just a few of my favorites that have helped me walk boldly out of what I was bonded to, and into the freedom that is life in the loving light of Jesus Christ:

"Come to me, all you who are weary and burdened, and I will give you rest. Take my yoke upon you and learn from me, for I am gentle and humble in heart, and you will find rest for your souls. For my yoke is easy and my burden is light." Matthew 11:28-30

"But if serving the Lord seems undesirable to you, then choose for yourselves this day whom you will serve, whether the gods your ancestors served beyond the Euphrates, or the gods of the Amorites, in whose land you are living. But as for me and my household, we will serve the Lord." Joshua 24:15

"I will instruct you and teach you in the way you should go; I will counsel you with my loving eye on you." Psalm 32:8

Maybe you have never practiced yoga, or even considered it. In that case, I hope I have spared you by going down that path with my sincere and honest story. I share it with the hopes that it serves as an example to how the world will offer seemingly good and pleasant options to replace Christ, and we must be cautious and careful to identify them and not pursue them, regardless how well-intentioned we think we are, or they are. Jesus is truly enough, and with Him, we really do not need "Jesus plus anything" to save us.

Establish Spiritually Healthy Routines

This is not to say we can't still seek what is truly good and pure for our bodies and souls in Christ. When we go through this healing process, and as we transform, I think it is a wonderful time to establish some spiritually healthy routines that involve the body and The Spirit. This is why I began working on a project called WorshipFlow, which is a faith-based alternative to Yoga. A practice that not only activates your body by flowing through soft stretches and balancing to worship music, but also helps us to be still in guided prayer, breathing, and meditation sessions on The Word. I still believe it is important for us to take a break from the busyness of our daily life in order to focus on His Will and get clarity, and to be intentional about this, even more intentional than I was about showing up to a yoga class ritually.

Another great habit I've gotten into, that anyone can do, is spend time daily in worship. Whether it is while I am doing the dishes in the kitchen, or on a "Spirit Walk" where I tune out all social media or other distractions and solely listen to worship and praise music, I think this is a wonderful way to heal. Spontaneous praise is truly a sweet, sweet sound to His ear. The more we lift Him up, the higher our souls and spirits will rise in union, or yoking, with Him as He heals us from the inside out.

I highly encourage you to try taking a daily "Spirit walk" to spend alone time with The Lord while getting your blood flowing. It's a routine I've begun by taking my prayer time to the streets, or trails. I will literally block out 45min to an hour, leave all of my tech devices at home, and tell my family "I'm going to take a walk with Jesus". Sometimes I really just need to go spend time outdoors, getting my physical heart rate up as I open my heart and soul up to God in prayer. There's something so liberating about being in His creation and celebrating Him. Don't be surprised if certain thoughts and prayers have you picking up your pace, and you suddenly realize you've conquered some serious distance and worked up a sweat! It's really one of my most favorite workouts that I can say involve both my body, soul, and spirit, and can be done almost anywhere at any time.

Leave The Past Behind

As we move into this realm of new creation and experience His healing, it's important to know that we confidently leave the wreckage and harmful things of our past behind us. For me it manifested in leaving people and a lot of nasty habits out of my life. Other physical habits I had to cut out and briefly mentioned before, but won't dwell on in depth, were: smoking, drugs, binge drinking, listening to and participating in gossip, clubbing, profane music, horror movies, running away with strangers to exotic places just to escape, and living in a literal land of delusional grandiosity. I came out of a really dark place that I dwelled in for over a decade while living in my twenties on South Beach in Miami. Anything and everything that you can imagine about that lifestyle of non-stop partying, jet-setting, and living the literal "high" life with drugs and alcohol while trying to keep up with the models and celebrities I was "friends" with, almost killed me.

If He can pluck me from the dens of iniquity that I had placed myself in by letting the enemy take the reins and closing my eyes and ears to the knowledge of His Truth that I knew deep within my soul, He can do it for you too. However, it does require truly letting go of what is in your past and holding you back, to give quite literally everything over to Him, surrendering all your fleshly will, and allowing Him to work His healing process over you.

Now to the soul and spirit:

We have dealt thoroughly with the body and healing with our physical intentions, but there is a deeper shift that is also taking place at the same time, and it is within the soul and spirit. This convicting shift has an effect on what we do or don't do with our bodies, and most definitely affects the deepest level of our beings as we constantly strive to come to a place of complete and total healing, from the inside out. So, as we continue to transform into our new selves, we sometimes need to do more than just "let go" of the past. Some of us carry toxic soul ties that actually need to be attended to, and broken, before we can truly enjoy the freedom of healing and forgiveness.

Break Toxic Soul Ties

Toxic soul ties might sound like something you hesitate to admit having, because who would willingly make them and carry them around aftersall? They come in different forms, and some are more obvious than others once you start looking for them. Let's begin with some of the easier ones to identify:

Are you holding a grudge, anger, or judgment against someone? Maybe they're holding it against you... Those can be toxic soul ties. If we spend our time and energy focusing negatively on what others have done to us, we aren't letting go and allowing God to occupy that space with His healing. It might sound impossible to do at first, so we can simply become mindful of those emotions for now, and write them down.

How about those painful memories from your past that haunt you, or even shame you? Yup, I have had several of those, and they can all be toxic soul ties. Write them down as they come to mind.

Now onto the less obvious ones: Soul ties can happen unknowingly, like while doing yoga poses and chants that open your soul to unknown spirits...Jot down any of these that might come to mind, and pray for God to open up His wisdom and discernment as you self-seek in this part of the journey.

They can also happen knowingly: Like your ex who you swore was your soulmate, and thus made a covenant with? Yup, lay them all down at His feet by adding them to your list as more toxic soul ties.

Chances are we all have toxic soul ties, in most categories, and the good news is WE CAN BREAK THEM! No longer does the burden of burying our past away need to be our means of daily survival or defense mechanism, for He has washed us clean. Lay your everything out, whatever thoughts, people, and actions that your past can negatively conjure up, and hand them over to Him.

Once you've got your list, here's some simple steps you can take to break those toxic soul ties:

1- PRAY & CONFESS "Father, I thank you for being ruler of my heart and all of the spiritual realm. I thank you, Lord, for knowing and breaking all of the toxic soul ties that I may have come into with the enemy, and Lord I ask for the ones I know of, and those I might not even know..."

2- FORGIVE "Father, help me to forgive those that have caused toxic soul ties and have hurt me. Lord, my heart cries out to you, and I forgive them..." Be specific now, call them out by name and by offense. Move down your list and call them out. Envision the person, place, or thing, and you let go of them (perhaps you can see a physical letting go happening in your mind). This will help you heal and free you of carrying it any longer.

3- REPENT & RENOUNCE, "Father, I declare and decree now that any covenant or agreement that I've made with these toxic agents of the enemy be broken in the name of Jesus. I thank you, Holy Spirit, for convicting my heart, and for activating the change in my body, soul, and spirit. Oh Holy Helper, give me Your wisdom and discernment to live out these changes, in Jesus Name!"

4- HEAL & RESTORE "Father, I thank you for freeing and healing my body, soul, and spirit from any elements this toxic soul tie has left. Make me whole and restore what the enemy has stolen from me. I surrender it all to You, Lord, my whole heart is Yours. Help me to love others with the same Christ-like love You show me.

In Jesus Name, Amen.

Trust In His Word

There are some verses that I dwelled in heavily to encourage His healing and restoration in my body, soul, and spirit during this part of the process that I want to share with you know:

"Therefore you shall lay up these words of mine in your heart and in your soul, and bind them as a sign on your hand, and they shall be as frontlets between your eyes. Deuteronomy 11:18

"And do not fear those who kill the body but cannot kill the soul. But rather fear Him who is able to destroy both soul and body in hell." Matthew 10:28

1 Corinthians 15:33 - Do not be deceived: "Evil company corrupts good habits."

Ezekiel 13:18 - This is what the Sovereign LORD says: What sorrow awaits you women who are ensnaring the souls of my people, young and old alike. You tie magic charms on their wrists and furnish them with magic veils. Do you think you can trap others without bringing destruction on yourselves?

Ezekiel 18:4 - For all people are mine to judge—both parents and children alike. And this is my rule: The person who sins is the one who will die.

Open up your heart to him fully and let Him in. There is nothing He doesn't already know, but there is a special kind of healing beauty that comes from handing it all over to the Father. There is a special feeling that happens when speaking them aloud as you hand them over into His hand, and let yourself just be held by His Loving Arms.

He has the whole world in His Hands after all, and He's got you. He can liberate you. He can heal you and He has forgiven you and can even help you forgive yourself. This is true freedom and liberation in His love. Give yourself extra grace and patience in this delicate phase of letting yourself be totally vulnerable while leaning into Him.

4 ACTIVATE

"And be not conformed to this world: but be ye transformed by the renewing of your mind, that ye may prove what is that good, and acceptable, and perfect, will of God."
Romans 12:2

By now, we have arrived at the place where we can rest in the comfort of His Hand, and have surrendered ourselves fully to Him in body, soul, and spirit. We have taken many steps towards making a dedicated effort of drawing near to Him, and this is how we reap the activation of the Holy Spirit. Now, we are in a place of true liberation from our previous bondages, both physical and spiritual, and we can truly seek Him in all that we do. As we move through this realignment, we can rest assured that as we renounce the superficial ways of the flesh and the world, our minds are renewed, and we activate what God has aligned for us in His perfect goodness. His will is proven to us and we see what is acceptable, clearly laid out for us.

Put On The New Self

I'll admit, there are definitely seasons where I find myself almost constantly battling the flesh. It can happen slowly, like swapping up my morning routine of spending time in The Word, and scrolling social media instead. Suddenly, I'm having all these comparison thoughts, gaining earthly desires, and even passing judgement. It doesn't take long for this type of seemingly innocent behavior to become a total thief of my joy. Then, it starts to affect the way I treat myself, and those around me too.

41

So yes, it does take a mindful and conscious effort for us to activate the "new self" that we have committed to and have fallen so in love with through Him, and to put away our earthly natures. Our aspiration can now realistically be that of a "lofty spiritual life" [2], where we confidently know that through Christ, we can rise above our earthly nature. There is such beauty in knowing that Christ is our mediator, at the right hand of The Father, and that we can come to him as we are. With pure hearts, despite often feeling filthy in our flesh, He can always make us clean again. We see this beautifully scripted out for us in His Word from Colossians Chapter 3 verses 1-17:

Therefore, since you have been raised with Christ, strive for the things above, where Christ is seated at the right hand of God. Set your minds on things above, not on earthly things. For you died, and your life is now hidden with Christ in God. When Christ, who is your life, appears, then you also will appear with Him in glory.

Put to death, therefore, the components of your earthly nature: sexual immorality, impurity, lust, evil desires, and greed, which is idolatry. Because of these, the wrath of God is coming on the sons of disobedience. When you lived among them, you also used to walk in these ways. But now you must put aside all such things as these: anger, rage, malice, slander, and filthy language from your lips.

Do not lie to one another, since you have taken off the old self with its practices, and have put on the new self, which is being renewed in knowledge in the image of its Creator. Here there is no Greek or Jew, circumcised or uncircumcised, barbarian, Scythian, slave, or free, but Christ is all and is in all.

Therefore, as the elect of God, holy and beloved, clothe yourselves with hearts of compassion, kindness, humility, gentleness, and patience. Bear with one another and forgive any complaint you may have against someone else. Forgive as the Lord forgave you. And over all these virtues put on love, which is the bond of perfect unity. Let the peace of Christ rule in your hearts, for to this you were called as members of one body. And be thankful.

Let the word of Christ richly dwell within you as you teach and admonish one another with all wisdom, and as you sing psalms, hymns, and spiritual songs with gratitude in your hearts to God. And whatever you do, in word or deed, do

---

[2] The Pulpit Commentary, Electronic Database. Copyright © 2001, 2003, 2005, 2006, 2010 by BibleSoft, inc., Used by permission

it all in the name of the Lord Jesus, giving thanks to God the Father through Him.

When we reroute our hearts and minds to the higher spiritual aspects versus the lowly earthly ones through Christ, we have activated Him within ourselves.

"Trust in the LORD with all your heart and lean not on your own understanding; in all your ways submit to him, and he will make your paths straight." Proverbs 3:5-6

If we meditate on His word and activate The Spirit in our life, then we gain a personal guide to fulfilling His will and His plan for us.

Psalms 1-4

How blessed is the man who does not walk in the counsel of the wicked,

    Nor stand in the path of sinners,

    Nor sit in the seat of scoffers!

But his delight is in the law of the LORD,

    And in His law he meditates day and night.

    He will be like a tree firmly planted by streams of water,

    Which yields its fruit in its season

    And its leaf does not wither;

    And in whatever he does, he prospers.

This can become a constant practice in your daily life, where you are re-routing former negative tendencies and patterns in thought and behavior, and supplementing them with prayer, meditation on The Word, and supplication. I am constantly calling on the Holy Spirit to intervene with

His wisdom and discernment when I face trials and tribulations, both big and small, in my day. Further, when I feel the snares of the enemy starting to tear at my mind or through others I cross paths with in my day, I will stop and immediately call him out and tell him to get behind me. His word says:

"Submit yourselves therefore to God. Resist the devil, and he will flee from you." James 4:7

Jesus turned and said to Peter, "Get behind me, Satan! You are a stumbling block to me; you do not have in mind the concerns of God, but merely human concerns." Matthew 16:23

Claim Your Godly Confidence

As you come across the enemy, do not fear, for the Lord has not given us a fearful spirit. Activate the victory you have been given in Christ over him and tell him exactly where to go. I sometimes literally say out loud "Get behind me Satan", or "Shut up Satan" or "Go to the pit of hell with your filthy self and your agents" outloud when I feel the enemy lurking.

It's a sweet life when we claim this Godly confidence and activate it. We learn that we can quite literally walk and talk with Jesus and His authority - all day, every day. We must also be mindful of our tongues, for they have the power of creation!

John opens his gospel with a masterful display of the power of His Word in Chapter 1 verses 1-3:

In the beginning was the Word, and the Word was with God, and the Word was God. He was with God in the beginning. Through him all things were made; without him nothing was made that has been made.

The Lord simply spoke creation into existence. A popular new age movement of "manifesting" has become widespread, where people have wrongfully been persuaded that if they simply begin to desire deeply for something, and speak it, it will be attracted to them in the universe, and it will come to them. We as believers know better. We know that we are working in and through the ultimate power, Him. We know that our flesh often has passions and desires that are completely opposite of what the Spirit wants. If we replace God with "the Universe" and start intentionally trying to manifest things on our own, we are basically telling God we don't need Him. We aren't seeking His will, but our own, and we aren't inviting Him to direct us in prayer and supplication, we are telling Him, "we've got this". This is the opposite of humility, our hearts posture when abiding in Christ, and the opposite of Godly confidence. It's purely pride. On the surface, many people don't see how dangerous that act of manifestation actually is, or what a true insult it is to our Father in Heaven.

Jesus's brother James writes on *"Taming the Tongue"* in Chapter 3 verses 3-8 of his book:

When we put bits into the mouths of horses to make them obey us, we can turn the whole animal. Or take ships as an example. Although they are so large and are driven by strong winds, they are steered by a very small rudder wherever the pilot wants to go. Likewise, the tongue is a small part of the body, but it makes great boasts. Consider what a great forest is set on fire by a small spark. The tongue also is a fire, a world of evil among the parts of the body. It corrupts the whole body, sets the whole course of one's life on fire, and is itself set on fire by hell.

All kinds of animals, birds, reptiles and sea creatures are being tamed and have been tamed by mankind, but no human being can tame the tongue. It is a restless evil, full of deadly poison.

Guard Your Tongue

As we begin to live more intentionally aligned with His spirit in our body, soul, and spirits, we must tame our tongues to be peace-makers, to speak wisdom, and to speak of goodness. We must refrain from cursing others, even when no one is around to hear, for we know God is infinite and the enemy lurks like a lion waiting to destroy. Don't give him a foothold!

With the tongue we praise our Lord and Father, and with it we curse human beings, who have been made in God's likeness. Out of the same mouth come praise and cursing. My brothers and sisters, this should not be. James Chapter 3 verses 9-10

What we sow we will reap, and we must dwell on what is good. Philippians 4:8 in the Amplified version reads:

Finally, believers, whatever is true, whatever is honorable and worthy of respect, whatever is right and confirmed by God's word, whatever is pure and wholesome, whatever is lovely and brings peace, whatever is admirable and of good repute; if there is any excellence, if there is anything worthy of praise, think continually on these things [center your mind on them, and implant them in your heart].

What we think, we will speak, and we can start taming our tongues by training our minds, and our hearts. We must fill them both with positivity, and resist that which is negative with all our might:

*Keep your **tongue** from evil and your lips from speaking deceit. Proverbs 15:2*

Remember, we don't have to rely on our own strength to do this. Life as a new creation in Him is a co-creative process where we are constantly transforming in Him and through Him. Rely on His Promises that He has given to us so generously in His Word.

Activate The Fruits Of The Spirit

We have a wonderful array of tools that have been gifted to us in the form of the fruits of the Spirit. We can and should pray for the activation of these gifts often:

Galatians 5:22-23 But the fruit of the Spirit is love, joy, peace, longsuffering, gentleness, goodness, faith, Meekness, temperance: against such there is no law.

Living our daily life can now look more like learning to constantly move and flow with Him, through these gifts. When we sense ourselves shifting away from the gifts of the fruits of The Spirit, we can mindfully and intentionally pause, and come back to them through prayer and supplication. I have this verse on my refrigerator, and they have become a sort of "self-mental checklist" where I can notice myself either in sync with what His will is for my life with their presence, or out of sync with His will by their absence. If I start to feel unsure or a certain way about a decision or action that I'm about to take, I run through the gifts and ask "is this aligned with these fruits of the Spirit". Chances are, if it's not, then it's not in His will for you. He wants us to act and live in love, in joy, in peace, he wants us to have the endurance that it takes to keep our cool and have patience in long suffering, He wants us to be gentle, good, faithful, humble and meek. These fruits have become excellent indicators for alignment, and I'll share more on that in Step 6, when we focus on being in position by having an abiding relationship as our way of life. Before we get there, I want to take some time to intentionally meditate on the importance of being still with the Lord.

5 BE STILL

Being still in the Lord does not mean becoming complacent, or lazy, for we are to constantly be transforming, from glory to glory, and letting Him take us into new places, new revelations, and new spiritual awakenings.

But we all, with unveiled face, beholding as in a mirror the glory of the Lord, are being transformed into the same image from glory to glory, just as by the Spirit of the Lord. 2 Corinthians 3:18

To me, this is the most divine way of experiencing life on earth: Being still with Him, meditating on His Word, and seeking Him in every single thing that we see, do, hear, breathe, think, and place we go. He is both omniscient and omnipresent, and when we stop running from Him (which is a futile effort because He is everywhere), and stop letting our flesh react (instead of letting Him act through us) we can share in his all-encompassing love, mercy, grace, and protection. This is when and where "the good stuff" happens.

Doing Life With Him

Life shared with The Holy One is truly the richest experience on earth, so this little sweet spot of being still, it's so much more than a passing moment, or blank mind (like we used to practice in worldly yogic meditation), or empty space; it is the fullest richest experience. It can only be done when we let ourselves go, and live fully in Him, and let Him live fully in us, so that when it's time to act, our flesh no longer "reacts". We are fully cloaked in His armor, and living in His abundant life, free from the redundant cycles of our own pasts. Jesus tells His disciples this in the Book of Matthew:

Whoever wants to be my disciple must deny themselves and take up their cross and follow me. For whoever wants to save their life will lose it, but whoever loses their life for me will find it. Matthew 16:24-25

We have discussed the Greek word for life used in this verse, "psuche" back in Chapter 1 when we discovered our beings as composed of body, soul and spirit, with "psuche" being the word for our soul and where our mind, will, and emotions dwell. In this phrase, the word is also being used to mean "breath". It is so wonderful when we take the time to understand the many uses of a word, and suddenly multiplied depth to a single verse can be revealed. Without breath, we know our bodies cease to have life. It is also so for our souls, without Him our souls are doomed to death, but as followers of Him, they have eternal life. It's abundantly clear that if we lay down our lives by devoting our entire beings in body, soul, and spirit to Christ, then we ultimately find His Peace that comes in the stillness of self, and fully trusting and obeying Him in all of our ways, for all of our days.

The mind governed by the flesh is death, but the mind governed by the Spirit is life and peace. Romans 8:6

Continually Surrender

We have already done a lot of intentional and active work in opening ourselves up, letting go, healing, and consciously activating our spirit with The Spirit. Here is the sweet spot, where we let go in surrender, and let Him do the work in us and around us. It can be done several times a day if we need to, and it only takes mindfully pausing and asking Him to do it for you in the same ways we already did in the previous steps. Why wait for it all to build up into what might become an issue and a problem? Now you know that you can stop and surrender to His stillness at any time, in any place.

If you're anything like me, that probably sounds a lot easier than it actually is to do. Here's where I share a little personal story that I'd rather leave unscripted but, for sake of total transparency, and that you might not have to experience such a thing… here we go: On the inside of my right arm I have the words tattooed "Be still and know that I Am…"And I actually had this put on after a spiritual awakening by God, but before I was fully walking with Him. It took the utter desolation, isolation, and abandonment of others, and even myself, for me to reach this point. This all went down in an international destination where I was a total and complete stranger to the world around me.

Remember how I said I would often run away to exotic places with total strangers? Well, this was one of those trips, only this time I was supposed to be meeting a friend, and I really thought I could trust this person. Things didn't exactly pan out like I'd planned, and instead, I was literally left with nothing, on the other side of the world, oceans away. They even had my passport at one point, and I did not have a penny, I didn't speak the language, I had no place to sleep…nothing. It was like a breaking point, where everything in my life seemed shattered, and instead of just lying there and giving up, relishing in the depression of desolation, (because let's be honest, sometimes that is the seemingly easier choice) I had a divine peace that surpasses all understanding. I remember looking up from the sand towards the blue sky and seeing the leaves move in the tree where I had taken refuge in the shade to lay my head, and I thought… This is it. This is the end of the road. I've run as far as I could possibly get on this planet, and I'm completely done. I'm completely alone. I have nothing. One stark and remarkable fact struck me: No matter how far I've come and what I've seen and done, I was never truly able to run away and lose myself. Here I was in brash reality: Just me, and God.

Instead of a total lack of desire or bleakness, which is what I maybe should've experienced in depression, or a false sense of energy from the adrenaline of knowing I was completely broken. Normally, I'd have this sense that I better jump up and start getting busy for the sake of "being busy". That I would be best to begin trying to fix my problems and figure out how I would eat, sleep, and eventually get home. Instead, I felt a peace that literally said "Be still", and for a while this was all I heard. I sat with this comfort and hope, and obeyed the command. After a while the full phrase "Be Still and know that I am God" came. Now, I knew that the peace I had felt and the voice that was ushering these words into my heart was God Himself, and that despite my wayward walk, and terribly selfish decisions that led me to where I was at that very moment, He would not let me break. More than anything, I needed to return to Him, and rest in Him instead of stirring up more of my own busy ideas and actions.

Avoid False Productivity

Maybe you know this false type of productivity that creeps in when you think if you just work harder towards something and pour all of yourself into it, that you're bound to climb upward and out of whatever funk you find yourself in. Well, if you've tried this, or like me, made a lifestyle out of it, you also probably know that this pretty much never works out the way we think or hope it will, and that's because we are the ones driving the ship, not Him. It's often a whirlwind of commotion that is just that, motion. We may think we are pushing ourselves forward, but once the dust settles, there's nothing of actual substance that was accomplished, and just the wreckage that we have now left behind.

In Proverbs 3:6 it says we are called to, "Acknowledge Him in all your ways and He shall direct your next step".

When I'm the one trying to direct my own steps, even when I am trying to walk with Him, I end up getting severely in my own way. Even worse, I find myself getting in His way. His divine path and purpose and plan for me becomes stalled because I'm fumbling the next step, albeit well intentioned. Now I know better, and I go back to the beauty of stillness, and being still in Him.

A wise mother of a rambunctious teen friend I had back in middle school once told me, "Misery loves company", as she found me left behind on a sleepover at their house where she had just caught the aforementioned friend sneaking out. She was referring to her own daughter, and warning me that if I kept on keeping such company, that I'd quickly find myself commiserating. From a young age I was told, directly or indirectly, that this is how important it is to have the moments of stillness (and better yet:

stillness with The Father), rather than running away from, or towards, something else. However, I kept on running away, and towards absolutely nothing, for decades. It took a culmination of several life-lessons and God-lessons that I had to learn the "hard way" to realize that "being still" was also so that, when it's time to act or react, we are fully cloaked in His armor. It's a time where we stop getting in our own way, where we are liberated, where freedom comes and sets in motion a divine series of actions and reactions that we no longer orchestrate, because we are letting Him work in us and through us, and a time and place where we can *finally stop being our own worst enemy*. David wrote a wonderful Psalm that rejoices in The Lord knowing our hearts, and searching us:

O Lord, you have searched me and known me! You know when I sit down and when I rise up; you discern my thoughts from afar. You search out my path and my lying down and are acquainted with all my ways. Even before a word is on my tongue, behold, O Lord, you know it altogether. You hem me in, behind and before, and lay your hand upon me. Such knowledge is too wonderful for me; it is high; I cannot attain it. Where shall I go from your Spirit? Or where shall I flee from your presence? If I ascend to heaven, you are there! If I make my bed in Sheol, you are there! If I take the wings of the morning and dwell in the uttermost parts of the sea, even there your hand shall lead me, and your right hand shall hold me. If I say, "Surely the darkness shall cover me, and the light about me be night," even the darkness is not dark to you; the night is bright as the day, for darkness is as light with you. Psalm 139:1-12

6 ABIDE

Now he who keeps His commandments abides in Him, and He in him. And by this we know that He abides in us, by the Spirit whom He has given us. John 3:24

On earth, Jesus often used the phrase "follow me" when speaking to His disciples. Shortly before He was ascending into heaven, he chose a different phrase. He extended an invitation to us by saying, "abide in me". Abiding in Him is more than just following Him, it means living in Him and through Him. Rather than mimicking or observing, like when we follow something, we are literally depending on Him and incorporating Him into all that we think and do. Abiding in Him is where we want to be if we are to stay in position throughout our lives and receive the fullness of His fruit-bearing gifts. It is also where we need to be if we intend to carry out His plans and purpose for us. We may have received the gift of salvation, but there is much more to our intended New Life with Him, as His new creations. If we aren't careful to honor the co-creative process of living life by abiding in Him, we can and will fall out of position.

In Faith, By Grace

When we unite with Christ through salvation, and we ask Him to forgive our sins and promise to obey Him, we begin an abiding relationship with Him. We become intimately aware of our new life, and receive the Holy Spirit to intertwine with our spirit. This is the beginning of a supernatural Oneness of life that we get to experience through Him while on earth. Through this, we learn to awaken our inner beings and transform them into

53

New Creations through Him. We allow Him to heal us from the inside out, activate the gifts of the Spirit, and rest in Him by being still with Him.

This type of abiding relationship is not actualized by our own strengths. In fact, the definition of abiding means to bear patiently, to endure without yielding.[3] In reality, it's much less us, and much more of Him that allows us to abide. In the last chapter I talked about the false productivity that comes out of us being busy to just be busy. Or, the destructive type of productivity that occurs when we happen to be getting in His way for us. When we are not walking with Him, this type of action can very quickly culminate into calamitous whirlwinds. However, it's also possible to do while we are walking with Him, and that is not what it means to abide, nor is that how we "gain our salvation".

Romans 3:23 says "for all have sinned and fall short of the glory of God".

Perhaps you have heard that one cannot be "saved by works" and that we are only "saved by Faith alone". It is quite literally impossible for any well-meaning Christian to earn their way into Heaven. That simply is not how it works, and thank God for that, because clearly, we all fall short. It was by His infinite grace and mercy that He sent His son as the ultimate sacrifice for our sins, and our faith in Him alone is how we are given the gift of Salvation.

This does not mean, however, that we are to just ride the wave of "salvation is by faith and not by works so I will abandon any effort of trying" while we are still here. James sums it up quite nicely in his bit on *"Faith and Works"* in Chapter 2, verses 14-26:

14 What use is it, my brethren, if someone says he has faith but he has no works? Can that faith save him? 15 If a brother or sister is without clothing and in need of daily food, 16 and one of you says to them, "Go in peace, be warmed and be filled," and yet

---

[3] "Abide." Merriam-Webster.com. 2021. https://www.merriam-webster.com (8 August 2021).

you do not give them what is necessary for their body, what use is that? 17 Even so faith, if it has no works, is dead, being by itself.

18 But someone may well say, "You have faith and I have works; show me your faith without the works, and I will show you my faith by my works." 19 You believe that God is one. You do well; the demons also believe, and shudder. 20 But are you willing to recognize, you foolish fellow, that faith without works is useless? 21 Was not Abraham our father justified by works when he offered up Isaac his son on the altar? 22 You see that faith was working with his works, and as a result of the works, faith was perfected; 23 and the Scripture was fulfilled which says, "AND ABRAHAM BELIEVED GOD, AND IT WAS RECKONED TO HIM AS RIGHTEOUSNESS," and he was called the friend of God. 24 You see that a man is justified by works and not by faith alone.

James the Just was portraying some of the very skills of parable storytelling here he might've learned from his brother Jesus to get an important message across. Faith is important and our works can't earn us a way into heaven, but we must also live out our Faith. In this instance, James gives the idea that there might be a brother or sister who has a desperate need for clothes and food, and they come to the trusted church body and reveal their needs, but instead of anyone helping them they're simply told "we will pray for you". Don't get me wrong, prayer is important, but so is opening up your pantry and closet, sharing your food and extra clothes with them. If the works are aligned with a real need and you see in your faith that this is what Jesus would do, and don't do it, but instead say you will hold your faith and pray for them, what good are you doing to show His righteousness here on earth? How are you truly spreading His Light and His Love as one of His disciples by simply saying "Have faith and stay strong" without actually helping? Thus, it's not enough to just say we have faith and go on living completely in the flesh. James says here that even the demons have faith. They know who The Lord is. So, it is not by faith alone that we must live if we want to activate His righteousness and grace in our lives, but through our faith and what we do because of it. Each and every day will bring new opportunities for us to act out our new creation, to approach situations with His righteousness and grace, and because of our faith, we will know which new way to act and put away our old self. I think this is why some wise minds have likened our faith-walk to a long-distance race. We want to finish strong, not burn out in the first leg. Remember, none of this is by our own will or strength, our faith-walk is a collaborative life long process involving living as Jesus did, with the help of the Holy Spirit, and in obedience to God The Father.

The Vine and the Branches

There is another beautiful parable in the Bible that illustrates what an abiding life-long relationship with Christ looks like, and that is of Jesus as The Vine. John 15, verses 1 through 12 say:

1 "I am the true vine, and my Father is the gardener. 2 He cuts off every branch in me that bears no fruit, while every branch that does bear fruit he prunes ᵃ so that it will be even more fruitful. 3 You are already clean because of the word I have spoken to you. 4 Remain in me, as I also remain in you. No branch can bear fruit by itself; it must remain in the vine. Neither can you bear fruit unless you remain in me.

5 "I am the vine; you are the branches. If you remain in me and I in you, you will bear much fruit; apart from me you can do nothing. 6 If you do not remain in me, you are like a branch that is thrown away and withers; such branches are picked up, thrown into the fire and burned. 7 If you remain in me and my words remain in you, ask whatever you wish, and it will be done for you. 8 This is to my Father's glory, that you bear much fruit, showing yourselves to be my disciples.

9 "As the Father has loved me, so have I loved you. Now remain in my love. 10 If you keep my commands, you will remain in my love, just as I have kept my Father's commands and remain in his love. 11 I have told you this so that my joy may be in you and that your joy may be complete. 12 My command is this: Love each other as I have loved you.

What a wonderful way to look at this new creation relationship that we get to live out for the rest of our lives. Jesus is the vine, we are the branches, and His Father is the gardener. For our branches to bear that fruit, we must remain in the vine (Jesus) and endure the pruning of The Father. It is to the Father's delight that we as the branches will bear much fruit, and Jesus tells us this again in the book of Matthew:

"Ye shall know them by their fruit." Matthew 7:16

We are not called to stress or have anxiety over how we are to keep abiding in Him. No, it is much more about surrendering to Him. If we surrender our entire beings (body, soul, and spirit), then He will give us the strength and courage to persevere in His ways. Sometimes, more wreckage comes about in a believer's life when they resist or create tension as Jesus is gently leading them in a certain direction that might be opposite of their fleshly desires. Therefore, if we simply give up, if we lay down our lives for Him, as He did for us, then we will experience life with Jesus as the Vine. But, our work doesn't stop there, we are also commanded to go out and bear fruit, and carry His word to others by example, by loving one another as He has loved us. We will go over more of this in depth in the last chapter.

Of course, this does not mean that we won't have those days where the enemy's lies just seem to torment our ears and minds. However, we now have the tools to overcome the enemy attacks, and we have boldy claimed the victory through Christ. I, for one, tend to have a lot of passion about things I become excited about, and especially about the things I love. God happens to be one of those "things" that I can really get lit up about, and sometimes I find myself feeling let down by my own lack of completion of works, or for falling short. My heart's desire, even well intentioned, will sometimes get me down if I start letting that thief of joy called comparison in. Suddenly, I'm looking at my goals and what I've been able to complete in a season, and comparing it to what I dreamed I'd get done, or worse yet, what someone else accomplished, and the anxiety and disappointment begins to set in. It's clear that we all will fall short of the Glory of God (Romans 3:23), so why do I let the enemy discourage me with his lies and tell me that I am not enough even though I am really trying to live in an abiding life with Christ? One way I combat this is by diligently taking joy in my salvation. There is nothing like ticking off the enemy with the sounds of praise to The Lord, and it is the most instantaneously effective mood booster and literal "lifter of spirits" that I know how to do. It's in a mindset like this that I am more likely to keep my peace and experience the fruits of the Spirit in my life. He is the vine, The Father is the gardener, and we are the branches. We must be diligent to claim and exalt our God-given fruits in this life.

Every good and perfect gift is from above, coming down from the Father of the heavenly lights, who does not change like shifting shadows. James 1:17

Beware Counterfeiting Christ

A lot of pagan rituals that counterfeit Christ by replacing Him, have become popular in modern culture. Some believers are falling into the trap and lure of subscribing to them, so I think it's worth taking a moment to mention a few here. As we continue on living life in The Way of His love, by putting God first, let's never forget that He is the source of all goodness. A myth that has become prevalent in recent days is that of crediting the "universe" for things that come our way instead of God. Maybe you've heard someone say "The universe just doesn't want me to have this right now", or "The universe is giving me signs". People often do this in order to soften the message of where true power comes from (Him), to avoid offending non-believers, and to get the point across that perhaps there is a power greater than us alone. This is so much more dangerous than it may appear at first, for it is robbing The Lord of the praise He is so worthy of. It is placing "the universe" and the belief that we ourselves hold any form of power outside of Him, as false idols. Although it is often done as a courtesy to non-believers, it's counterfeiting Christ, and no courtesy is worth that.

The heavens declare the glory of God, and the sky proclaims the work of His hands. Psalm 19:1

Another trap some well-meaning believers fall for is astrology as a "supplemental guide" to their lives. It might seem harmless to start learning about horoscopes and relying on astrological signs, in addition to prayer. Perhaps studying the planets and stars for when they align seems intriguing, but what comes next is often the weighing of decisions based on what we find. If we are using these as guides to life, instead of His Word, even supplementally, it is counterfeiting Christ, for it is replacing Him in the seeking. Instead of relying on Him, we're seeking signs in creation, and not The Creator:

Lift up your eyes on high and see who has created these stars,

The One who leads forth their host by number, He calls them all by name;

Because of the greatness of His might and the strength of His power,

Not one of them is missing. Isaiah 40:26

The universe, the stars, the planets, they all exist because of Him and are under His command. The universe is not full of anything other than what God has created. Think about that for a moment. Literally, every single thing out there, is under His command. Why would we counterfeit His power by seeking answers outside of Him? Why would we give credit or worship to anything other than the Creator? He has made it known that there is no inherent power in the stars, planets, and endless space that is frolicking to and fro between the heavens and earth. Even more, we know that the devil is the Prince of The Air and that he lurks in those spaces; they are his domain.

Job 1:7 "Where have you come from?" said the LORD to Satan. "From roaming through the earth," he replied, "and walking back and forth in it."

Crystals, oils, and incense are other things I have previously misused. Crystals are undeniably one of God's gorgeous creations, and the book of Revelation cites part of the New Jerusalem will be built from them:

It shone with the glory of God, and its brilliance was like that of a very precious jewel, like a jasper, clear as crystal. The wall was made of jasper, and the city of pure gold, as pure as glass. The foundations of the city walls were decorated with every kind of precious stone. The first foundation was jasper, the second sapphire, the third chalcedony, the fourth emerald, the fifth sardonyx, the sixth carnelian, the seventh chrysolite, the eighth beryl, the ninth topaz, the tenth chrysoprase, the eleventh jacinth, and the twelfth amethyst. Revelation 21:11, & 18-20 NIV.

At first, I had only appreciated them for their beauty, but as I began to slip deeper into my new age spiral, I started to learn about specific stones and their "healing properties". I started buying chakra stones for healing certain parts of my spirit and body. Again, I never really thought this was a total conflict to my Christianity, or that I had clearly crossed the line into what was known as pagan magic, or even witchcraft, in the Old Testament:

"When you enter the land the Lord your God is giving you, do not learn to imitate the detestable ways of the nations there. Let no one be found among you who practices divination or sorcery, interprets omens, engages in witchcraft, or casts spells, or who is a medium or spiritist or who consults the dead. Anyone who does these things is detestable to the Lord." Deuteronomy 18:9-12 NIV

I seemed to be able to deny the fact that I was hoarding them in my house like some sort of shrine, and attributing powers to them as if they'd possibly bring heaven down to earth. Again, I got into these on my slippery slope downward. I did not start out believing in certain powers for certain stones, but by the end I was practically praying to them. I bought and made jewelry which I wore on my neck and around my wrists to ward off or attract certain "energies" or spirits. There's a verse that directly addresses this, and if only I had known then, I could've avoided the pitfalls that came from opening up my spiritual gates to this occultic stuff.

"This is what the Sovereign Lord says: 'Woe to the women who sew magic charms on all their wrists and make veils of various lengths for their heads in order to ensnare people. Will you ensnare the lives of my people but preserve your own? I am against your magic charms with which you ensnare people like birds, and I will tear them from your arms; I will set free the people that you ensnare like birds. I will tear off your veils and save my people from your hands, and they will no longer fall prey to your power.' " Ezekiel 13:18, 20 & 21 NIV.

I had both invited and allowed for a total body, soul, and spirit penetration by dark magic that I never saw coming from the start. Likewise, another more subtle yet abused substance in mass market consumerism and modern culture today is essential oils. There's an entire industry that accredits properties well beyond their creation's intent, which I believe is to be pleasing to the nose and natural medicinal properties. For example, tea tree oil is a wonderful antiseptic and anti-inflammatory. I believe God created a plethora of natural medicinal properties as part of His works here on earth, but I think it ends there. A specific oil cannot and should not be used to attract abundance, wealth, or ward off evil. Unfortunately, there are plenty of well-known MLM companies out there swaying the minds of well-intentioned homemakers who can make their "own business" out of hustling these and along with it, influence others to believe that these oils can work any sort of magic outside of smelling good or specifically treating what their intended medicinal herbal use is. This is falsely associating God's power to His creation. We worship the Creator, not His creation.

I also practiced smudging as a ceremonial rite, and it involved burning sage to cleanse the soul and ward off evil. Most people are familiar with burning incense, and it's true that it has been used for thousands of years. People use it for their aromatherapeutic pleasures, and personally, I think that's fine. However, if you are attributing any "sacred properties" to specific herbs with the intent of cleansing your soul, ridding your home of evil, and warding off negative energy or spirits, than I would highly caution you to pray for The Holy Spirit to reveal His wisdom and discernment unto you.

We must be conscious about misplacing our trust, our praise, and our worship into the creation, versus The Creator. We do not want to replace Christ, with creation. Recall that deception is literally the devil's oldest trick in The Book, when Satan deceptively convinced Eve to eat the fruit of the Tree of Knowledge. The devil still uses the same old trick today, convincing us what we know is wrong by making it look right or feel good. Sadly, it still works.

I am afraid, however, that just as Eve was deceived by the serpent's cunning, your minds may be led astray from your simple and pure devotion to Christ. 2 Corinthians 11:3

Instead of allowing ourselves to follow the whims of what others say is harmless, or that which our flesh might immediately desire, we can instill His righteous ways by installing routines that evoke joy in Him, and by Him. Instead of waking up and checking what the stars might have in store for us today based on our astrological sign, we might try a Bible devotion instead. We can come to the throne room with our questions and concerns about what lies ahead, instead of seeking any type of truth from these other sources.

I knew a mother who was also a believer, and she and I were pregnant around the same time, only she had to battle cancer and go to chemotherapy throughout her pregnancy. I recall watching her lose her hair and become completely bald as her belly grew bigger and I would weep for her and her unborn child as well as pray for her strength to persevere. Prayer warriors rallied up for her from all over the world, and she stayed strong in her faith and fought that nasty disease. Not only did she beat cancer, but she also gave birth to a totally healthy baby girl. About 6 months later, she shared something that I think she must've thought was totally harmless, because she said so. She said, "When I am unsure of what is to come next, I consult a psychic from home, it's cheap and easy, and so, why not?!" I was stunned. Even on my most slippery slope, I still never went there. But having gone to loads of other seriously dark places with my incredibly wrong decisions in life, I wasn't judging her. I was legitimately concerned for her. She had just won a severe battle against death and disease, and brought fresh life forward in faith. Why would she summon this stuff up and invite it into her life?

There is a part in the Old Testament that I find really interesting, when King Saul visits a medium to raise Samuel's spirit. This isn't interesting to me because Saul decided to visit a psychic, but because it actually worked. Samuel rises, and rebukes Saul for disturbing him. Saul wanted him to foretell future events of whether he would have victory in a battle or not. What Saul tells him instead, is that because of his disobedience to God, both he and his sons would die the very next day. See, the Bible doesn't tell us that this stuff isn't real. In fact, it is very real, and dangerous, because it opens pathways to the spiritual realm that we end up in warfare over, and unnecessarily so. 1 Samuel 28:3-20 tells us how *"Saul Consults a Medium"*

Now Samuel had died, and all Israel had lamented for him and buried him in Ramah, in his own city. And Saul had put the mediums and the spiritists out of the land.

Then the Philistines gathered together, and came and encamped at Shunem. So Saul gathered all Israel together, and they encamped at Gilboa. When Saul saw the army of the Philistines, he was afraid, and his heart trembled greatly. And when Saul inquired of the Lord, the Lord did not answer him, either by dreams or by Urim or by the prophets.

Then Saul said to his servants, "Find me a woman who is a medium, that I may go to her and inquire of her."

And his servants said to him, "In fact, there is a woman who is a medium at En Dor."

So Saul disguised himself and put on other clothes, and he went, and two men with him; and they came to the woman by night. And he said, "Please conduct a séance for me, and bring up for me the one I shall name to you."

Then the woman said to him, "Look, you know what Saul has done, how he has cut off the mediums and the spiritists from the land. Why then do you lay a snare for my life, to cause me to die?"

And Saul swore to her by the Lord, saying, "As the Lord lives, no punishment shall come upon you for this thing."

Then the woman said, "Whom shall I bring up for you?"

And he said, "Bring up Samuel for me."

When the woman saw Samuel, she cried out with a loud voice. And the woman spoke to Saul, saying, "Why have you deceived me? For you are Saul!"

And the king said to her, "Do not be afraid. What did you see?"

And the woman said to Saul, "I saw a spirit ascending out of the earth."

So he said to her, "What is his form?"

And she said, "An old man is coming up, and he is covered with a mantle." And Saul perceived that it was Samuel, and he stooped with his face to the ground and bowed down.

Now Samuel said to Saul, "Why have you disturbed me by bringing me up?"

And Saul answered, "I am deeply distressed; for the Philistines make war against me, and God has departed from me and does not answer me anymore, neither by prophets nor by dreams. Therefore I have called you, that you may reveal to me what I should do."

Then Samuel said: "So why do you ask me, seeing the Lord has departed from you and has become your enemy? And the Lord has done for [b]Himself as He spoke by me. For the Lord has torn the kingdom out of your hand and given it to your neighbor, David. Because you did not obey the voice of the Lord nor execute His fierce wrath upon Amalek, therefore the Lord has done this thing to you this day. Moreover the Lord will also deliver Israel with you into the hand of the Philistines. And tomorrow you and your sons will be with me. The Lord will also deliver the army of Israel into the hand of the Philistines."

Immediately Saul fell full length on the ground, and was dreadfully afraid because of the words of Samuel. And there was no strength in him, for he had eaten no food all day or all night.

Guarding Our Gates

How many times have you ever heard the phrase "Open doors invite"? We must guard our doors, which are our spiritual gates. They are built into our bodies, and controlled by our souls (our minds and desires), and they can give direct access to our souls and spirits when opened. Our eyes, ears, mouths, minds, and hearts need to be actively protected. When we open them up to fleshly passions and desires, or even worse, divination, witchcraft, and other dark forces, we cannot simply blame the devil when things begin to go awry. Sometimes it is our own flesh, and our own fault for not exercising the self-control that we know is a spiritual fruit in our possession. We have the power and authority to activate His Word, and to turn ourselves from victim to victor through Him. We have been called to follow Christ, and can simply abide in Him, with The Father, and have The Holy Spirit in us.

Enact The Fruits of The Spirit

Like fruit on the vine, we hunger and thirst for His righteousness, and we desire Him like fresh living water that gives us new life. Restoration and renewal is what He promises as gifts for following and abiding in Him. Our constant struggle against our flesh can be countered with declarations of self-discipline. This is how we enact the fruits of the Spirit, which are beautiful blessings from above, and divine gifts that give us the ability to oppose our fleshly ways when abiding in Him.

Galatians Chapter 5 verses 16-25 says this about *"Walking by the Spirit"*:

So I say, walk by the Spirit, and you will not gratify the desires of the flesh. For the flesh craves what is contrary to the Spirit, and the Spirit what is contrary to the flesh. They are opposed to each other, so that you do not do what you want. But if you are led by the Spirit, you are not under the law.

The acts of the flesh are obvious: sexual immorality, impurity, and debauchery; idolatry and sorcery; hatred, discord, jealousy, and rage; rivalries, divisions, factions, and envy; drunkenness, orgies, and the like. I warn you, as I did before, that those who practice such things will not inherit the kingdom of God.

But the fruit of the Spirit is love, joy, peace, patience, kindness, goodness, faithfulness, gentleness, and self-control. Against such things there is no law.

Those who belong to Christ Jesus have crucified the flesh with its passions and desires. Since we live by the Spirit, let us walk in step with the Spirit. Let us not become conceited, provoking and envying one another.

Discipline is also essential in training, and we are training for a life-long walk with God. We gain strength as we exercise this spiritual fruit of self-control and we gain endurance to both finish strong and have an abundance stored up to pour out when needed. It also keeps us in position to both give and receive His love, and His perfect will and plan for our lives.

Prayer and Devotion

One of the most healthy and fruitful routines I have gotten into is my morning devotionals. Before my eyes even fully open, I'm reaching for my Bible. Some days I roll out of bed and go straight to the floor where I greet the day with praise and worship music as I let Him lead me through His Word. A sacred moment where I am purely allowing Him to tune me for the day, to set the tone for what He has in store for me, and to honor Him and know that I can trust Him to carry me through whatever it may be.

Do not be anxious about anything, but in every situation, by prayer and petition, with thanksgiving, present your requests to God. And the peace of God, which transcends all understanding, will guard your hearts and your minds in Christ Jesus. Philippians 4 verses 6-7

Strike anxiety down at the moment it begins to rear its ugly head in your life, and be sure to say "thank you" when you ask the Father your requests. So many times, we start our prayers with our "asks" instead of leading with praise, rejoicing, and gratitude. Think about it. If it was a phone call and you had this one friend who called you every day and always started out with "Can you do this favor for me?" … How would you feel? Our Father loves us, and we are His children. He delights when we speak to Him, so let's be a little more intentional of how we go about it and practice at least the very same manners we would expect to receive from a friend on a phone call, shall we?

As we become bolder in our faith walk with Him, we will come across trials and tribulations of the enemy. This is something that, in essence, reaffirms how He is moving through us, and that we have become fierce in faith. The devil loves the lazy, because they are a sitting duck, an easy target, and they have no desire to do God's work, so they pose no threats against him as he conducts his evil business. In 2 Thessalonians Chapter 3 verses 1-10 Paul writes a letter to both request prayer, and warn the body of believers there to not remain idle:

Request for Prayer

As for other matters, brothers and sisters, pray for us that the message of the Lord may spread rapidly and be honored, just as it was with you. And pray that we may be delivered from wicked and evil people, for not everyone has faith. But the Lord is faithful, and he will strengthen you and protect you from the evil one. We have confidence in the Lord that you are doing and will continue to do the things we command.

May the Lord direct your hearts into God's love and Christ's perseverance.

Warning Against Idleness

In the name of the Lord Jesus Christ, we command you, brothers and sisters, to keep away from every believer who is idle and disruptive and does not live according to the teaching [a] you received from us. For you yourselves know how you ought to follow our example. We were not idle when we were with you, nor did we eat anyone's food without paying for it. On the contrary, we worked night and day, laboring and toiling so that we would not be a burden to any of you. We did this, not because we do not have the right to such help, but in order to offer ourselves as a model for you to imitate.

For even when we were with you, we gave you this rule: "The one who is unwilling to work shall not eat."

Being lazy is something that is much easier to do than taking action, you catch little flack by keeping to yourself. You also reap what you sow, so, if you're sowing nothing, you're reaping...nothing. When you answer His call to go out and truly love one another, spreading His love, and His Word, you can catch some flak for sure, and if not from the people you are trying to love on, then surely the enemy will rise up with other trials for you. Again, it's all a part of the process and while it is not something we necessarily rejoice over, we can counter it with a whopping dose of prayer, and go straight to the Lord with praise and worship, for there is no sound like a praising mouth and heart the enemy detests more. It will drive him right away.

The Armor of God

Sometimes, however, we have an all-out spiritual war going on. This is when the enemy doesn't just launch one attack, but he seemingly has declared warfare on you and your loved ones. Again, we have the victory in Christ, it has already been claimed, so it's important we understand how to adorn ourselves in the Armor of God when we go out to get fierce in our faith and battle-ready! Ephesians 6 verses 10-18 says this:

Finally, be strong in the Lord and in his mighty power. Put on the full armor of God, so that you can take your stand against the devil's schemes. For our struggle is not against flesh and blood, but against the rulers, against the authorities, against the powers of this dark world and against the spiritual forces of evil in the heavenly realms. Therefore put on the full armor of God, so that when the day of evil comes, you may be able to stand your ground, and after you have done everything, to stand. Stand firm then, with the belt of truth buckled around your waist, with the breastplate of righteousness in place, and with your feet fitted with the readiness that comes from the gospel of peace. In addition to all this, take up the shield of faith, with which you can extinguish all the flaming arrows of the evil one. Take the helmet of salvation and the sword of the Spirit, which is the word of God.

And pray in the Spirit on all occasions with all kinds of prayers and requests. With this in mind, be alert and always keep on praying for all the Lord's people.

Putting on the full armor of God means we need to fully understand, and claim, His spiritual blessings for us. There are seven pieces in total and we will walk through how to understand and activate each of them.

First, is the Belt of Truth. Think for a moment about where a belt goes, it's worn around your waist, and it surrounds you at your very core. It also keeps all the other pieces of armor in place. It is central and of utmost importance to being fully battle ready. This means we need to be keenly aware of surrounding ourselves in His Truth, which we find in His Word. We spoke about speaking life and being wary of our tongues, so start there, and begin to speak His Word in your day, throughout your whole day, and pray to Him unceasingly. I find myself talking to God so often these days that my teens no longer even ask "Mom, are you talking to yourself?", because they already know. They've come to respect me for it, at least I think, because I will go bold. I mean something can pop up and I'll go off into the Spirit and they'll be like "woah okay, she's on top of it", but really, He is on top of it, and there's nothing better than being the one your family or loved ones think to petition first when they need help raising up prayers.

Second, the Breastplate of Righteousness covers our most vital organs. It is there for protection when we might not have our other weapons up and receive an unexpected blow. We are to saturate ourselves in our innermost beings with His righteousness. And what exactly is His righteousness? It is His perfect way of doing things, and again, this is found in His Word, and in Jesus's perfect character. Have you ever heard of the movement WWJD? When I was younger, the bracelets were super popular and our church gift shop sold them. I used to try and purchase a new one every Sunday, if my parents would let me, so I could have an arm full. It stands for "What Would Jesus Do?", and honestly, I wish someone would bring those back, because they are excellent reminders right there on your arms to think about how He would act before you react to things in your daily life. This is a wonderful way to activate His Righteousness, by being more like Him. We can also use the fruits of the Spirit here to run though again as a checklist and make sure that whatever we are aligned in love, joy, peace, patience, kindness, goodness, gentleness, and self-control. These are all aspects and characteristics of righteousness.

Third, is the shoes of the Gospel of Peace. What a sacred and precious piece of armor this one is. We can literally use spreading the Gospel of Peace as a weapon. Think about that. We can counter evil attacks, with His peace. Sounds like the old hippie slogans "make love not war", and really maybe they were on to something, but they were activating a worldly and lustful love that goes awfully awry. We, however, have His everlasting and eternal love and peace to activate that actual carries the power of salvation wherever we walk. In Roman times, their shoes were more like sandals, and other than having thick soles to protect the bottoms of their feet, they also had spikes that would help them brace for a blow and stand firm in their foundation. Just like the spikes on the bottom of a Roman sandal, we can activate the Gospel of Peace as our firm rock and foundation, wherever we go.

Fourth, we have the Shield of Faith. This is a giant piece of weaponry that acts as our first and ultimate defense against the enemy. It is both large, and in charge, when wielded. It helps us remain steadfast and bold, remember, you are fierce in faith and when you activate it, no weapon formed against you shall prosper, and your faith will serve as an anchor for your soul. Proclaim His word:

No weapon that is formed against thee shall prosper; and every tongue that shall rise against thee in judgment thou shalt condemn. This is the heritage of the servants of the LORD, and their righteousness is of me, saith the LORD. Isaiah 54:17

"We have this hope as an anchor for the soul, firm and secure. It enters the inner sanctuary behind the curtain". Hebrews 6:19

Have you ever watched an ancient battle scene in a movie, where they all line up and make these impenetrable shield walls out in the middle of a battlefield? Well, that's because we are stronger in numbers, and when a believer stands firm in union with another, in the Body of Christ, it can be like one of these massive and intimidating boundaries that we can create against the enemy. Don't suffer alone in silence and be bold enough to entrust a member of the Body of Christ to pray and stand with you in battle.

Fifth is the Helmet of Salvation, and we all know a helmet is worn on your head. Our heads are also what the enemy would love to strike down first, because they are the most vulnerable parts of our bodies. We can fight without an arm, without a leg even, but a good blow to the head and we will surely fall. Recall what gift we all receive upon Salvation, the Helper, the Holy Spirit and His indwelling in us. We must be headstrong in our conviction of the Holy Spirit, and call upon Him to lead us and guide us. When we wear the Helmet of Salvation, we already know that not even death can conquer us, for we have received Christ and the promise of everlasting and eternal life with Him. It kind of defeats the enemy flat out with that right there, doesn't it? Like, what can he even do? Kill you? That's no longer a fear. Removing the fear from death is such a powerful gift to live the rest of your life with, and not only that, it's the ultimate liberation from any temptation or tactic the enemy can toss your way. It's the highest card in the deck, it's your ace of spades card, and you can pull it out and flash it his way at any time, reminding the enemy who you belong to and in whose power and authority you decree and declare your salvation.

Sixth, we have the Sword of The Spirit, and what a mighty weapon this is! The other pieces of armor all act as defensive, but the sword is one that is used actively to pierce straight through joints and marrow. In Hebrews 4 verse 12 it says:

For the word of God is living and operative and sharper than any two-edged sword, and piercing even to the dividing of soul and spirit and of joints and marrow, and able to discern the thoughts and intentions of the heart.

Thus, in the Spirit, we can activate the wisdom and discernment to understand the thoughts and intentions of the heart, and this works both for our own selves, and for others. If you sense deceit, strike back with the Sword of the Spirit and activate His wisdom to give you the insight and clarity to act out His Word. We have His Word, and scripture, as the ultimate weapon against the enemy. Saturating ourselves in scriptures and being truly intentional about the time we spend daily in The Word will help us be better equipped when it comes time to wield our Swords of the Spirit. If you find yourself in the heat of an attack, verbally call upon the Word of the Lord and say "Your Word says…". He knows what He has said, and He will listen.

Seventh, is our lifeline that keeps us going throughout it all, and that is Prayer. If we want to fight with His victorious power and authority, then we surely cannot do it on our own. Only through fervent prayer and supplication can we be saturated enough to let what we have stored up in Him pour out in a battle. Don't be lazy in this task of saturation, be joyous as you do it, be steadfast as you seek Him, and speak to Him constantly. Remember how I said don't lead with your ask when coming to the Lord in prayer like a bad friend on the phone? Well, another thing to activate in prayer is impulsivity. As our relationship with Him grows, our conversations are likely to become much more spontaneous with Him. Let your talks to God sound like one with a best friend, where you have no idea where you might go with it, and you don't even think twice about how you begin it, you just pour yourself out. It's really fundamental in a lifelong abiding relationship with God, and we will surely see and feel His presence as we do. A great place to look for examples of this is the Book of Psalms, where King David and others pour out their hearts to the Lord without holding back. Just about every emotion can be found in that beautiful book, and it should encourage us to feel confident we can do the same even now.

This is such a precious gift of intimacy, the abiding relationship that we get to enter into with The Father by way of His son. It is something that is worth rejoicing over daily, multiple times a day! Through rejoicing and spending time being still with The Lord, we become saturated in His presence with His Word. When the time comes to pour out the overflow and abundance of His goodness, we become living vessels of His love. Aligning our will with His will, our mind with His Purpose, and totally surrendering our souls, we can obediently and honor Him as we both move and stay still... As Reverend Andrew Murray so eloquently says in his book, "Abide in Christ", it is a "wondrous oneness of life and interest". I highly recommend reading it if you'd like to take a deeper look at living out an abiding relationship with Him.

7 LOVE ONE ANOTHER

A new command I give you: Love one another. As I have loved you, so you must love one another. By this everyone will know that you are my disciples, if you love one another
John 13:34-35

Jesus has called us forth with a command, and it is a law of love. Let's break this down and fully grasp what it means to love one another as He has loved us. By doing this, we may be known as His disciples.

Once we have become conscious and committed to intentionally living life with Jesus as the Vine, it's easier for us to envision how we can carry out His command to love one another. Like abiding in Christ, this can be misperceived as something of a task or chore. Surely, some people are harder to love than others, and some situations in life will push us to the very brink of our faith, but it is still possible to surrender it over to His love. When walking fully consecrated to the surrender in Christ, seeking His will and not our own, and being obedient, this type of love becomes our very nature. It is also the key to living a truly happy life with unparalleled joy and peace.

We are being commanded to love as He loved us, and that type of love is not the worldly type that comes and goes. No, it is the unconditional type that lasts, through thick and thin, through highs and lows. This might conjure up a familiar and traditional ceremonial vow of marriage: "I, _____, take thee, _____, to be my wedded wife/husband, to have and to hold from this day forward, for better, for worse, for richer, for poorer, in sickness and in health, to love and to cherish, till death do us part, according to God's holy ordinance; and thereto I pledge thee my faith." Of course, marriage is a serious matter, and the heart and soul of a person spends a lot of time considering the brevity of devotion that a commitment to one another like this has. However, what if we were able to bring our whole hearts to the table when we vow our lives to Christ? To walk with Him for the rest of our lives, and to put all of our faith in Him even more than we do in any man or woman?

Worldly Love Vs. Godly Love

I messed this one up pretty severely in my own life. I went on a decade-long hunt looking for love in all the wrong places, and fully committing to it. What I hadn't done, was completely consecrate myself to God. Instead, I was looking for a person to fill this hole in my heart and life. I ended up falsely convincing myself that I had found the one, more than once, and utterly devoting my entire life, emotions, body, and being, to these people. I was fully trusting that they would carry me to the next place I needed to be in life, or that we could get there together if they just believed in me enough and I worked hard enough to earn their love. All the while, I was totally ignoring any personal type of relationship with God.

These relationships were centered around selfishness, indulgence, lust, and lies. Yet, I poured all of myself into them, thinking something great could possibly come out of it because I had invested so much of my heart and soul into them. You can imagine, when I began to realign with Him and got to the step of breaking soul ties, just how many I had to break. To be totally honest, I still do. When the Lord reveals them to me He will remind me in a dream with someone I haven't thought of in a long time, or in a random thought that arouses a memory in the middle of my day. I will stop and pray for that person, asking for forgiveness, and for God to break my soul ties with them. That is how reckless I was with my most precious possessions, my heart and soul, in my former way of life. That is also how important the need to be loved is, it strikes to our very core. I just had to learn the hard way, more than once. In order for me to find true love, I had to lose myself. First, surrendering totally over to Him, so that I could come to learn what His true love meant (and there is no truer love than that). Secondly, so that I could then heal enough to realign in body, soul, and spirit. Finally, I could love another, fulfilling the command to "love on another". This spans way beyond a partner relationship, and reaches into every aspect of how I deal with the outside world. However, I see now, that trying to find or keep even one honest and true relationship without these things at the foundation, was for me, inherently doomed.

I once heard a wise person say, "Trust no man, but trust the Jesus in man". Knowing that we are called and commanded to love one another regardless of their humanity, and despite their own flawed human nature, as He so loved and loves us, we can start to see just how unconditional and pure, and also how liberating this new way of life through love is. We no longer need to seek conditions that are worthy of our love, best behavior, or favor. We simply default to love, and let Him take care of the rest. Matthew 6 verse 33 says, *"But seek first the kingdom of God and His righteousness, and all these things will be added to you."*

Branches of His Love

If this sounds a little too lofty to you, or wonderful in thought but not in practicality, then perhaps we can understand how to do this a bit better using the same parable we talked about previously: Jesus as the Vine. We discussed having Him as our vine while learning to abide in Him, and that we are to bear His fruits as branches. In John 15, verses 13-17 He explains this further. It is written:

Greater love has no one than this: to lay down one's life for one's friends. You are my friends if you do what I command. I no longer call you servants, because a servant does not know his master's business. Instead, I have called you friends, for everything that I learned from my Father I have made known to you. You did not choose me, but I chose you and appointed you so that you might go and bear fruit—fruit that will last—and so that whatever you ask in my name the Father will give you. This is my command: Love each other.

We are an inseparable union. We are both dependent on Him to receive the living water, and He depends on us to carry forth the fruit we as branches bear, and share it with the world. It's a gorgeous union of purpose and will. We cannot exist without Him, without His power in us, we have no righteousness. Likewise, He relies on us to share Him with the world around us. Again, I have to reference Reverend Andrew Murray's book,

"Abide in Christ" for he covered this so powerfully in a couple chapters of his short book. On page 18 he says: "Without the vine, the branch can do nothing", and, "Without the branch, the vine can also do nothing. A vine without branches can bear no fruit". If we are willing to meditate over concepts like this, to read and digest them over and over, then we can unpack their wisdom, revelation, and they have the potential to be life-changingly huge.

Reverend Andrew Murray says, "So close is the union of the vine and the branch, that each is nothing without the other, that each is wholly and only for the other" (page 18, Abide in Christ) . Wow, just pause there for a moment. He is your beloved, and you are His. Wholly. That alone pulls at the very core of my heart strings. Walk through this thought with me for a moment:

The Creator of the Universe loved you so much that He sent His only Son to die for you, to liberate you from the bondage of sin and death, and He loves you enough to continue to carry you through with fresh living water daily, giving you all that He has access to through the Father.

Just as He gives us literally all of Himself, we are called to give ourselves wholly unto Him, surrendering to His will and purpose for our lives while unconditionally loving others. Here is the part that most of us, I think, can get wrong if we aren't careful to dwell and meditate on it… It is not a chore or task that we have to strive to fulfill, it is fully an honor.

Like the abiding relationship that is not achieved or maintained through any strength of our own, but a surrendering unto Him, so is this relationship of carrying forth the fruits he has borne unto us. It is quite literally accepting our position as abiding, in that sweet surrender where He holds us near, and allowing Him to keep us there, that gives us the energy and desire to go out and share it with others. Experiencing peace, joy, and love in this most pure form is not something we want to keep only for ourselves, we want to share it with our loved ones. This type of living vessel of living in and spreading His love is the key to ultimately aligning our bodies, souls, and spirits.

Humility As A Heart Posture

Thus, our call to live life with Christ on earth can be simplified as: Love God and abide in Him, and love one another as He loves us.

"And he said to him, "You shall love the Lord your God with all your heart and with all your soul and with all your mind. This is the great and first commandment." And a second is like it: You shall love your neighbor as yourself. On these two commandments depend all the Law and the Prophets." Matthew 22:37-40

I will be the first to admit that love was not, and still is not, always my default language. The soul, our will and emotions like pride, anger, pain, and fear can make some situations seemingly impossible to express love in. This is when we really need to exercise the self-control that we are gifted through The Spirit, and take refuge in Him. Fully trusting that He will hear our prayers, search our hearts, and guide us in the path towards a peace that surpasses all understanding so that we can meet some of life's toughest times, and people, with the agape love of God, rather than our own wretched flesh.

Let me tell you, my flesh has been mighty wretched. Is there anything less attractive than a person puffed up with pride? I'm not talking about the type of pride that one has for their loved one or child when they rejoice in a job-well done. I'm talking piety. The type of pride that comes adorned with entitlement, embellished with delusions of grandeur, and laced in ignorance. A lot of this worst version of myself came via a product of my environment and what I was currently worshipping: a high-paced high-life full of people, places, and things that exonerated worldly lusts and luxuries, and completely missing the meek and simple things. My key to escaping this was finding humility.

Do you know the phrase, "Those who live in glass houses shouldn't cast stones?" Well, to be honest, my path to humility looked a lot more like a crashing fall, myself utterly shattering from inside my glass palace atop an ivory tower. I had to totally and completely become exposed, in full filth. More than that, I had to break into a million pieces so not even with my best public relations efforts could I hide or conceal it, like I had anything left to put together in my life at all. I had to totally and completely break.

"Pride goes before destruction, a haughty spirit before a fall." Proverbs 16:18

I'm sharing this because humility doesn't have to be learned the hard way. There are several warnings and instructions that we can seek in His Word, and signs that can trigger us to stop and literally pause to seek God in the peace and quiet of our prayers.

A Living Sacrifice

There is a spirit of entitlement that accompanies pride. One that is coated in lies and deceit, and it tells us exactly what we think we would want to hear: That we are good enough, that we deserve better, that we can and should have everything our hearts desire, and at any cost. It has even become a common practice in the world, to rehearse such thoughts, declaring them in affirmations and chanting them over and over into the "universe" to manifest them. I was completely guilty of this for a time, and we have talked about that in a previous chapter. Selfish self-affirmations really are that dangerously destructive, because eventually they do work to "trick your mind" and train your core beliefs. You see, we will ultimately become what we worship. These thoughts when rehearsed and chanted over and over eventually become worship, and soak to our very souls by leading our minds to that false elevation point where we've convinced ourselves of the lie that we are as high and mighty as God. A place where we believe that we are worthy of claiming and proclaiming what we want for our lives, rather than seeking His will. We start to fully believe that we are in control instead of completely surrendering to be obedient to His perfect plan, and that we should be praised for our accomplishments while robbing God of His glory. Soon, the self is deluded, consumed in self-seeking promotion and self-love.

I wish I could say that I hadn't already known that we are to love God first and foremost when I practiced life this way. I knew this, I was raised hearing this. Alas, we do ultimately become like what we worship. I was so deep in the practice of self-worship and treating my body like it was a sacred temple to my own self, using yoga and self-love mantras as excuses to be completely indulgent and gluttonous with the blessings of abundance that I took for granted in my life. I will be the first to admit that my highest self, the most idealized version of me, is not worthy of worship. Not even a little bit. I am far better to worship God from whom all good things come from.

Furthermore, the teaching that our body is a temple actually came from the Bible, but the New Age world has tried to reclaim it as their own, and replace the temple of God, as the temple of the self:

"Do you know that your body is the temple of the Holy Spirit, who is in you, who you have from God, and you are not your own." 1 Corinthians 6:19

What happened when I stopped treating my body like I was just out here living my best life (a worldly famous yolo mindset), and stripped myself of any "fomo" (fear of missing out), I quit acting like I was some divine shrine to my highest most self-actualized being with a "flawless aura". I had broken it all, I shattered and destroyed that false altar I had created out of myself, and I laid it down as an offering. I, myself, became a sacrifice to the Creator. The one who gave me life and everything good, and promises that His plan will always be for me. And it was in this very space that I experienced the sweetest most liberating peace that surpassed all understanding. That peace, that love, that joy that comes from knowing that I am wholly His, and no longer had to suffer at my own hands, is still what motivates me. It is that space, that feeling, that firm belief and hope in Him, that keeps me going today.

Of course, I don't always find it easy to love myself, or even others. Life can, and does, still get in the way. When I find that ugly old nature trying to rear its head inside me, I turn to His word, plus a whole lot of prayer. I do have a fiery spirit, and I always have. It is something I used to propel me in my athletic career as an adolescent, and carried me to some great opportunities as an adult that I probably would have otherwise been overlooked for. I grew up with a common comment by almost all of my teachers and mentors on my personality, that I should pause and think before I speak. Basically, if I had an inkling of feeling something, or thinking something, I was saying it aloud. You can already imagine how this might not have always played out so well. Many times I found myself unexpectedly thrusted into a situation where deep emotions were flying, even hate, and it was all because of my own tongue.

We spoke previously about James the Just, and how he gives us some great direction on how to guard our tongues. He also gives great advice on how we might be least likely to experience wrath:

My dear brothers and sisters, take note of this: Everyone should be quick to listen, slow to speak, and slow to become angry". James 1:19

If we are careful and thoughtful listeners, we are more likely to choose our words carefully. If we become speakers of carefully chosen words, then we are also more likely to be patient and reflective. We just may find that it is easier to forgive others for their words from this position, before the feelings become words, that become actions, that become entire situations we could have avoided. I am ever recalling, in moments like this, that the goal is to spread love, and not escalate anything to wrath, or worse: hate.

I know a lot of things and events led up to Jesus Christ being at the cross, and that it truly was His divine mission for which He was sent here to earth. But, when it comes to the brevity of situations like I just mentioned, where my fiery passion begins to flare inside me and I have the urge to lash out, or even harder, lash back at someone who is already provoking me, I have to pause and think that it is quite possible the entire situation at the cross could be summed up in two words: man's hate. It's not just a coincidence that this Great Commandment that Jesus left us with as He ascended back into heaven was to love, for the consequence of *not loving* is *truly dangerous*. His blood washed us clean, and it set forth a path to peace for all nations and ages. It was His sacrifice that paid the highest price, and for that, I owe Him every good effort that I have to love first. To foremost greet my own soul and spirit with love, and to share that with others even if I'm struggling with my own flesh or others and really don't feel like it at the moment.

79

Ephesians 4:23- 32

Therefore each of you must put off falsehood and speak truthfully to his neighbor, for we are all members of one another. "Be angry, yet do not sin." Do not let the sun set upon your anger, and do not give the devil a foothold.

He who has been stealing must steal no longer, but must work, doing good with his own hands, that he may have something to share with the one in need.

Let no unwholesome talk come out of your mouths, but only what is helpful for building up the one in need and bringing grace to those who listen.

And do not grieve the Holy Spirit of God, in whom you were sealed for the day of redemption.

Get rid of all bitterness, rage and anger, outcry and slander, along with every form of malice. Be kind and tenderhearted to one another, forgiving each other just as in Christ God forgave you.

We are called to love wholeheartedly and sacrificially like God loves us. When we come to the sweet spot of being fully active and awake in our spirit with His spirit, and abide in Him, this commandment of loving wholeheartedly becomes our very nature. It becomes both what we reap, and what we sow. Surely, this is the reason He left it as our greatest commandment of all, for it is the key to joy and fulfillment in the physical and spiritual realm. Once we have worked through each of these steps, we might find that it's necessary to rework some of them at times, and some steps may need to be reworked more than others. However, this last step of Loving One Another is one that we want to constantly be living out as part of new creation nature in Christ.

Loving one another as He loves us is truly the secret to living a life ultimately aligned in body, soul, and spirit.

Made in the USA
Monee, IL
01 February 2022

90437514R00059